JAMAICAN COOKING

140 ROADSIDE AND HOMESTYLE RECIPES

Written and Photographed by
Lucinda Scala Quinn

Macmillan • USA

MACMILLAN
A Simon & Schuster Macmillan Company
1633 Broadway
New York, NY 10019-6785

Library of Congress Cataloging-in-Publication Data

Quinn, Lucinda Scala.
Jamaican cooking: 140 roadside and homestyle recipes / written and photographed
by Lucinda Scala Quinn.
p.   cm.
Includes index.
ISBN 0-02-861001-6
1. Cookery, Jamaican.   I. Title.
TX716.J27Q56 1997   97-1001
641.597292—dc21   CIP

Manufactured in the United States of America

10 9 8 7 6 5 4 3 2 1

JAMAICAN COOKING

FOR JENNY

WILL YOU QUENCH ME WHILE I'M THIRSTY?
WOULD YOU COOL ME DOWN WHEN I'M HOT?
YOUR RECIPE DARLIN' IS SO TASTY
AND YOU SURE CAN STIR YOUR POT
SO STIR IT UP LITTLE DARLIN', STIR IT UP
COME ON AND STIR IT UP LITTLE DARLIN'
STIR IT UP

—BOB MARLEY, 1972

CONTENTS

ACKNOWLEDGMENTS

Many thanks to all the wonderful Jamaican cooks whose food I've eaten over the years. Same to the most generous family of Sheila and Tony Hart, especially Bruce, my intrepid guide-interpreter. Appreciation to the Pinto family for years of graceful hospitality, especially those Christmas brunches! For food and guidance, thanks to Audley, Flo, Carl, Daryll, Hopeton, Maga, The Front-line Massive, Miss Christiana, Thelma and the incomparable Miss Lammie.

For Jamaican shelter and comfort, thanks to Mrs. Edith Desnos for her Blue Mountain hideaway, Silver Hill; Sally and Jason Henzel at fabulous Jake's in Treasure Beach; Willie Fielding at Oristano in Bluefields; Leroy and the Blue Harbor Hotel in Port Maria and the whole gang at Woodstock Farm (thanks Mary!).

To friends up north, Pam Moss, 'nuff respect for the righteous original graphics lining these pages. Hats off to Sunburst, Jamaican travel experts George and Judy Patsolas. Thanks to Girlfriend, who also got the vibe along with George, Rose and Scala bro's. L & k to Calder, Miles and Luca for patience and understanding during all those grueling (not!) research trips and taste tests and to Michelley and Nuy for making it possible. To Richie, my bedside editor and husband, you make "everyting Irie."

Thanks to the whole crew combined from Nolan-Lehr Co.'s, especially Karen, Donald and my agent, Carla Glasser, without whose "cred" this book might not have left the filing cabinet.

INTRODUCTION

As it has with so many visitors before me, Jamaica slowly crept into my soul through the years by exposure to its beautiful land, people and culture. This book is a fan letter, a thank-you note, an invitation and an introduction.

Summing up the sometimes intangible grip the island of Jamaica holds, British naturalist Phillip Henry Gosse wrote in his *Gosse's Jamaica 1844–45*, "But the picture itself, the thousand things that cannot be enumerated, birds, insects, flowers, trees, the tone of the whole, the sunlight, the suffused sky, the balmy atmosphere, the variety of foliage, the massive light and shadow, the dark deep openings in the forest, all, new, rich and strange."

Picture such a backdrop for a cooking style that springs from the many traditions that define Jamaica's culture today—Arawak Indian, Spanish, African, English, Creole, East Indian, Middle Eastern, Mexican and Chinese. The cuisine is an outgrowth of this eclectic population mix combined with Jamaica's bountiful local products, which thrive in its lush landscape.

The Arawaks, Jamaica's first known inhabitants, were said to consume in one week what the conquering Spaniards ate in a day. Aside from fish and shellfish, corn, cassava and callaloo are a few mainstays of the Arawak diet that survive today in recipes such as bammy and pepperpot soup.

The Spanish brought various fruits like plantain and citrus. The dish that today is known as escoveitch fish comes from their *escabeche* or pickled fish preparation. As the Africans from many countries began to arrive as slaves, so did many of their indigenous dishes such as ackra and fufu. Fortunately, the geography was similar to West Africa, which enabled the production of familiar crops like yam and corn. Traces of English influence are everywhere—from pickled meats and salted fish to desserts called puddings that are more like cakes.

The culinary history gets more complex with the postslavery influence from the new wave of indentured laborers from East India, China and the Middle East. Curries, sweet-and-sour preparations and Syrian dishes, such as *kibbeah,* exist in today's Jamaican cooking. Creole contributions like patties came during the days when troops were enlisted from other West Indian islands for various war efforts.

The tenacious Jamaican Maroons, runaway slaves of the Spanish and British who fled into the island's rough mountainous interior and eventually won the right to self-government, originated the jerk tradition by hunting and preserving wild hogs with pimento, peppers and ash.

Jerking is a prime example of necessity creating tradition. To fully understand the evolution of Jamaican cuisine, one must also consider the difficult conditions under which much of the food was cooked and consumed. The majority African slave population had few protein resources and was forced to rely on plantation masters for moderate amounts of salted fish, which were blended with their staple vegetables. As cooks, they tended to the culinary needs of the Spanish and English table, which further contributed to today's hybrid preparations.

What survives is a national cuisine that stands on its own, yet it is often obscured under the label of Caribbean cooking. It isn't Cuban or Creole food, rather it is a unique style that has emerged from the island's personal history. Authentic Jamaican food, when it is cooked with understanding, nourishes the body, mind and soul.

So many foods and dishes are named from the rich language of the Jamaican people. All around the island are hand-painted signs that announce jerk centers, fish and bammy shacks, fruit vendors, groceries, etc.—all with the most clever and inventive names, an invitation to any passing traveler.

Beckoning from any roadside are great cooks like Chef Irie of Annoto Bay in the Parish of St. Mary, a notorious seaside vendor who sells steamed fish and the rich golden broth known as fish tea at his self-named "human service station." Against the sound of rolling surf, a steady stream of local folks and travelers pull up by car or wander over on foot at lunchtime. An intoxicating scent, both sweet and saline, wafts from the gently simmering pots.

The infamous, indigenous Jamaican barbecue known as jerk thrives in the jerk mecca of Boston Beach in Portland. The road curves gently, leading out of town toward Boston Beach, where clouds of barbecue smoke billow from the jerk enclave. A spicy smell of burning pimento wood fills your nose. Strong, primitive wood structures house three jerk pits, each offering a variation on the same fare: jerk pork, chicken and sausage, roasted breadfruit and festival. This is a man's world. The meat is chopped, weighed and doused in spicy jerk sauce, eaten with sweet, crispy festival and washed down with cold Red Stripe beer. Reggae music pulsates in the background.

In the bustling capital city of Kingston is Hopeton's Best Jerk Chicken at Northside Plaza. This popular, late-night jerk stop has been doing business in the same spot for fourteen years. Three partners divide up seven nights during the hours of 4 P.M. to 4 A.M. Propped up on the curbside is a fifty-gallon drum, halved on a stand, that forms the grill with a cover. The smoke pours out of a makeshift chimney. Next to the grill a small table holds a round lignum vitae board for chopping the meat. Farther up the corner is a pushcart that sells the necessary drinks and cigarettes.

Kingstonians from all walks of life stop in throughout the night, some taking the jerk to go, others standing around eating and chatting while a colorful group of characters hangs out nearby.

Roadside jelly coconut vendors, such as Daryll in Kingston off Old Hope Road, sell this product to a constant stream of regular customers—with the price varying according to one's ability to pay. He says some people even come and get it for the hospital to be used in an intravenous drip because of its high fat, mineral and vitamin content. For fresh coconut water known as Ital Coolaid, the top of a green coconut is expertly hacked off and served with a straw. Afterward, with a chip of the shell, you can eat the soft jelly inside for its concentrated nutritious goodness and sweet, sensuous texture.

Roasted yam and salt fish is featured at Melrose Hill on the road to Mandeville in Manchester, a famous roadside stop where cars pull over to be greeted by someone holding a piece of brown paper underneath a chopped, roasted yam and a small piece of grilled salt fish. It's eaten by taking a bite of roasted yam and nibbling off a tiny piece of the grilled,

salted fish. The soft, smooth-textured yam is a perfect taste counterpoint to the chewy salt fish. The yams look like large logs sitting on top of the fire. Hanging from the rafters over the grill are fresh ears of corn, which are husked and roasted directly over the fire.

Beside a gorgeous, undeveloped beach on the south coast at Bluefield's Bay in Westmoreland is Julie's Meals on Wheels, an old bus with no wheels, which is known for its roast turbot fish. It is a popular stop for overheated road-weary truckers who travel the road connecting Kingston to Black River and Sav-La-Mar. The turbot fish has a dense, sweet-tasting flesh that is protected during cooking by its thick, leatherlike skin. Stuffed whole, it is laid over a metal griddle on a fire and periodically doused with a buttery liquid. Next to the grill stands a large soup pot filled with brewing fish tea. The soup combines pumpkin, chocho and green banana with the turbot for a thick, chowder-style consistency.

For a taste of the world-famous Blue Mountain coffee, visit the source by traveling up the narrow, winding roads that creep up into the Blue Mountains. Waterfalls spill out of mountain crevices. Tall trees with dense foliage form canopies over the glistening, rain-soaked bodies of local folks, who walk slowly with bunches of bananas balanced gracefully overhead. Sacks of coffee beans lie on the edge of the road. Men cut bamboo. A bright blue-painted hut on the hillside offers a cup of fresh Blue Mountain coffee. In the higher landscape, which is more lush and jungly, mist gently rises off the mountain tops only to be shadowed by a floating cloud. Tall, moss-covered trees boldly tower over the increasingly narrow road. Little pink wildflowers sprout from the banks of greenery. In the cool air, large fir trees thrive, juxtaposed against the long, perpendicular branches of bamboo. Long flaps of banana leaves bend overhead. From the peak, meadows appear as the view opens grandly onto the majestically sloping valleys.

Shrimp ladies sell bags of pepper shrimp in Middle Quarters in the Parish of St. Elizabeth—but for that story and more you've got to turn to the recipes and start cooking because "who feels it knows it," as the late Jamaican reggae artist Bob Marley sang. Anyone who has been to Jamaica and fallen in love with the local food will agree!

JAMAICAN ROADSIDE FOOD SIGNS

Lagwood Lawn Restaurant

Ocean Sweep Restaurant

Big Bird's Jerk Centre

Blue Nymph Bar

Bluefield's Jerk Centre

The Pork Pit

Winnie's Kingfish Kitchen

Top of the Line Bar

Chat Bout Drink Stop

The Big Apple Restaurant
and Pub

Little Dis Little Dat Grocery

Horselips Bar and Grill

Mi Yard Yard Style Restaurant

Straight Talk Excitement
Jerk Pork

Translove Sweets and Pastries

Marlene in the Morning

Love Bird Pub

Uncle's Fish Corner

Happy Hunter Jerk Centre
and Bar

Pick's Restaurant & Lounge

Roots Club and GoGo Dancing

Genus 'n' Shack

Top Taste Chicken Centre

Beanie Man Vegetarian
and Fruit Soup

Minnie's Herbal Restaurant

Bowe's Fish Spot

Finga Licken Jerk Chicken

Belly Full

Centre Pole

Little Chilsea Jerk Centre

Almond Tree Hot Spot

Dandy Shandy New Talk Bar

Old Man's Corner Bar

Teena's Exotic Seafood Bar

Mr. Delicious Jerk Chicken

Godfather's Pub

Challenge Fast Food

Sharon's Beer Joint

First & Last Tavern

Lady Beck Tavern

Life Savor Restaurant

Lloyd's Jerk Centre

Swaby Lake View Pub

Highway Jerk Centre

Neville's Curry Goat Joint

Falcon Crest Fish Centre

Golden Touch Jerk Chicken

Rose Bud's Bar

The Bean Stock Jerk Plus

Scuba Fresh Fish Depot

NOTES TO THE COOK

This book is intended to be useful for anyone from anywhere who might be interested in cooking some basic Jamaican dishes. It is aimed at Jamaicaphiles rather than at experienced Jamaican cooks, whose intuitive talent isn't available from any book. One must taste, smell and experience that first hand.

This is not intended as a definitive guide on Jamaican food but rather as a collection of some of the more popular dishes that have been eaten over the years.

I've purposely omitted recipes for a few important Jamaican dishes due to the unavailability of some ingredients abroad. For example, a dish called Matrimony requires star apple, which is only available in Jamaica three months out of the year.

I have not attempted to cover such dishes as Cow Cod Soup or Stewed Sea Puss—if you're craving either one, I suspect you already know how to cook it or where to go to eat it, and anyone else would probably grimace at the thought of it. One notable exception is ackee and salt fish, which is Jamaica's national dish. Canned ackee is available in some places, although banned in others.

There is a strong vegetarian or "Ital" component to Jamaican cooking, which is an outgrowth of the Rastafarian movement. It traditionally utilizes only the "fruits of the soil" in a natural, vigorously flavored preparation style that originates from African ancestry. The herb ganja is used liberally as a culinary spice. I've included a couple of Ital preparations that only scratch the surface of this highly evolved cooking style. The Rastafarian way of life is explored from a culinary standpoint in other books written by Rastafarians.

Jamaican cooking is exquisite in its simplicity. There are no big secrets (well, except maybe in jerk sauces). Most of these recipes are written from memories of delicious meals prepared by a wide range of cooks over the years. I've tailored most of the recipes down to the essential ingredients in keeping with the frugal, efficient nature of Jamaican cooking.

Where possible I've pointed out certain nutritional advantages of different ingredients because I believe so much of the healthy Jamaican spirit can be credited to the ingestion of good food, eaten in proper meals, shared with family or friends in a culture that still holds these values in esteem. Some of the elements, such as ginger, are also deeply rooted in the tradition of folk medicine, which is still practiced in some form by many Jamaicans.

Most of all, Jamaicans are great eaters who enjoy each other's company and generously share their spirit through the necessary function of eating and cooking. Regardless of one's economic level, dishes such as rice and peas or pumpkin soup are dear to the hearts of all.

Enjoy cooking from this book with the same flexible and open-minded attitude that is embodied in the Jamaican culture, and remember the national motto, "Out of many one people," which also sums up its culinary tradition.

INGREDIENTS AND PROCEDURES

One of the beautiful things about the Jamaican way is the easygoing attitude that pervades all aspects of life. "No problem, mon" or "soon come" are often-heard phrases that carry into every level of activity. Cooking is no exception. There aren't any complicated ingredients, procedures or equipment necessary for Jamaican cooking. The basic flavoring components should be available at most local markets.

Most of all, try to have a casual approach to the recipes, allowing yourself to substitute ingredients and improvise with equipment when necessary. Here are some explanations and substitute suggestions to help along the way. I am only listing those items that may not be readily discernible or that may require some special explanation.

ALLSPICE, also known as pimento berries, has a taste of cinnamon, cloves and nutmeg combined. It is best used by grinding it fresh from the whole dry berries as needed, although any commercial powder is an acceptable alternative.

BAMMY is a cassava cake that is rarely made at home. It's sold in Jamaica by bammy ladies on the roadside and is available at many markets. It can be ordered directly from Jamaica by contacting Tropical Truffles Limited, 17 Kingsway, Kingston 10, Jamaica W.I.

BROAD BEANS can be used fresh or dried. Also known as butter beans, they are similar in shape and taste to lima beans, which also make a fine substitute.

BUTTER OR MARGARINE can be replaced by vegetable shortening or lard when called for in pastry recipes.

CALLALOO is a leafy green that is similar in taste to Swiss chard or spinach and is cooked in the same way. Along with pak chow (bok choy), it's the main leafy green vegetable consumed in Jamaica.

CHICKEN is a staple meat in Jamaica. Like so many things on that wonderful island, for some reason the taste of chicken is particularly excellent, a far cry from the commercial varieties available in America. One rarely buys chicken already cut in pieces as Americans do. It is better to buy a whole bird for many reasons: It's usually cheaper and fresher, and the bony parts make a flavorful broth or seasoning for beans. A whole chicken is easily jointed by using your hands to guide you to the right spot and slicing off the legs, wings and thighs right in the middle of the joints with a very sharp knife. The breast is then split in half down the center and separated on both sides of the back bone. Chop the tips off the wings. Reserve the back, neck and wing tips for another use, such as chicken broth, which is made by boiling the parts together with salt and water for 1 hour.

CHOCHO is a vegetable also known as chayote and christophine. It is sometimes referred to as a vegetable pear because of its shape. Ranging in color from green to white, the prickly skin is peeled off before cooking. Its flesh, which is similar to cucumber, takes on the flavor of any accompaniment. It's usually available in Spanish markets.

COOKING OIL refers to any mild oil such as safflower, corn, peanut or vegetable oil.

COCONUT MILK is called for throughout the book, and it gives an ordinary dish, such as rice and peas, a truly unique flavor. The grating of the coconut flesh is a common sound in a Jamaican kitchen. It's very simple to make and is far superior to canned coconut milk, which is, nonetheless, a fine substitute when diluted with a little water. Here is a recipe for fresh coconut milk.

MAKES 2 CUPS

1 coconut
2 cups hot water

Crack the hard outer shell of the coconut with a hammer. Separate the flesh from the shell. Shred the flesh in a blender or food processor or by hand with a cheese grater. Pour the hot or boiling water over the grated coconut and let stand for 5 minutes. Pour it through a fine mesh strainer. Squeeze the remaining milk out of the flesh. It is now ready for a recipe.

GINGER is used in both a fresh and powdered form throughout this book, as Jamaica produces some of the world's finest ginger. Store a jar of powdered ginger on hand in the cupboard. Fresh ginger will keep in the refrigerator for a long time.

GREEN OR UNRIPENED BANANAS are eaten boiled, served as "food" alongside many main dishes and used for porridge and pudding. In my opinion, they are similar in taste and consistency to Irish potatoes, which I use as an alternative to green bananas in certain recipes.

PAWPAW (PAPAYA) grows widely throughout Jamaica and is exported. It is not as big as the Mexican papaya. The fruit and leaves contain a tenderizing element, which can render the toughest meat tender with a few drops of its juice. The unripened, green pawpaw is often used in chutneys and salads. The fully ripened pawpaw is eaten fresh and used in drinks. It is yellowish and soft to the touch when fully ripe and will keep in the refrigerator for up to five days.

PICKAPEPPA SAUCE, bottled in Jamaica since 1921, is known internationally for its unique flavor and quality. It is called for in some of the recipes and is a terrific table sauce to offer along with this food. It's widely available in most commercial groceries.

PLANTAINS are green bananas, different from sweet bananas, although they also sweeten as they ripen. Jamaicans slice and fry them for a side dish when they're ripe and use them in tarts and puddings. When plantains are fully ripe, their skin is almost completely black.

RED PEAS refer to beans that are commonly known as kidney or French beans.

RUM in Jamaica is a subject that could fill a whole book. Its history began when the British started commercial production from sugarcane soon after their occupation of Jamaica in the mid-seventeenth century. White rum, also known as "white lightning," is a clear liquid, which is used by many Jamaicans medicinally. For the purposes of these recipes, any golden Jamaican rum is preferred over rum produced elsewhere.

SALT COD (OR SALT FISH) has become an integral part of Jamaican cooking through years of use out of necessity. Originally it was added to vegetables as an affordable source of protein. Today ackee and salt fish is Jamaica's national dish. Salt cod (or salt fish) is widely available throughout the world.

SCALLION is sometimes spelled escallion in old Jamaican references. It is a main ingredient in jerk sauce and, along with thyme, forms a base for many dishes. The variety in Jamaica is much drier than what Americans are used to, with a more concentrated flavor. Either way you should always have scallions on hand when cooking from this book.

SCOTCH BONNET PEPPER is the primary pepper used in Jamaican cooking and is also a key flavor ingredient. It is so named for its resemblance to a Scottish tam. It comes in a range of colors from green—which is known as ripe and has an intense flavor and lower heat—to yellow, red, orange and brown, which are hotter. It is a close cousin to the Mexican habanero chili. They are available at Spanish groceries and are becoming more and more common in markets that carry specialty peppers. Although they are grown throughout the Caribbean, Jamaican Scotch bonnets are in a class by themselves, flavorwise. Be very careful when handling these lethal peppers. Always wash the knife, board and your hands immediately afterward. If the peppers are impossible to find or you're caught without them on hand, be sure to have a good bottle of Scotch bonnet hot sauce on hand in the cupboard. Use 1 teaspoon of sauce where 1 pepper is called for. There are several brands available in groceries as well as through mail order. My favorite brand is Busha Browne's Pukka Hot Pepper Sauce, which is now available at many supermarket chains. Inquiries can be made to Busha Browne's Company Ltd., Twickenham Park, P. O. Box 94, Spanish Town, Jamaica W. I.

SORREL refers to the red petals of a plant that belongs to the hibiscus family. The petals are dried and used in sorrel drink, a punch that is popular during the holidays. It is also used in jams and jellies. Specialty markets that cater to East Indians often sell it in small plastic bags.

THYME is the main savory herb in Jamaican cuisine and is often sold in Jamaican markets tied up with a bunch of scallions as a seasoning package. It can be used by the sprig, either fresh or dried, and removed before serving. Commercial varieties of dried thyme leaves available in small jars are also acceptable.

WEST INDIAN PUMPKIN (CALABAZA) is a large, irregularly shaped gourd that can be purchased in smaller pieces. American pumpkin or squash, such as acorn or butternut, are acceptable substitutes.

SAVORY SNACKS AND SIDES

COCONUT CHIPS

The sturdy texture of coconut makes it ideal for chips. People devour these snacks when served with cocktails. The coconut flavor really shines through when toasted.

1 coconut
1 teaspoon salt
2 teaspoons light or dark brown sugar
½ teaspoon ground white pepper

Preheat the oven to 350°F. Crack the coconut and drain the water. Remove the flesh from the hard shell. Peel off the brown skin from the flesh. Cut into thin strips.

Toss the coconut pieces with the salt, brown sugar and white pepper. Spread the coconut chips on a cookie sheet in one layer. Bake the chips until they are a deep golden color, about 10 minutes. Serve hot or cold.

CONCH FRITTERS

MAKES 12 FRITTERS

I've eaten these in different shapes and forms all over the Caribbean. They're a popular appetizer that should be served with a choice of sauces.

½ pound conch
Juice of 1 lime, plus ¼ teaspoon grated lime rind
½ cup all-purpose flour
1 teaspoon baking soda
1 teaspoon baking powder
½ teaspoon salt
¼ teaspoon freshly ground black pepper
1 egg
¼ cup milk
½ teaspoon Worcestershire sauce
2 teaspoons tomato sauce or finely diced tomato
2 tablespoons finely diced sweet red pepper
½ Scotch bonnet pepper (any color), seeded and minced
¼ cup vegetable oil

Wash the conch meat in the lime juice. Chop it in small pieces and cook in a medium-size sauce pan, covered in water. Bring it to a boil and simmer for approximately 2 hours or until it is tender. (It will still be chewy.)

Combine the flour, baking soda, baking powder, salt and black pepper in a large bowl. In another bowl, beat together the egg, milk and Worcestershire sauce.

...nd tomato sauce to the dry ingredients and beat until
...Stir in the sweet red pepper, Scotch bonnet pepper, lime

...e skillet over high heat until it is very hot. Drop small
...nto the hot oil. Allow the fritters to cook until bubbles
...½ minutes. Flip them over and continue to cook until
...wn on both sides. Blot off the oil with paper and serve
...uce.

...in advance and reheated in a 350°F oven for 10 minutes. Or you
...ute.

...pping sauce such as chutney or cocktail sauce.

CHOCHO FRITTERS

**MAKES 12 TO 14
FRITTERS
(4 TO 6 SERVINGS)**

These remind me of Chinese scallion pancakes, so I like to serve them with a soy dipping sauce. Chocho is a pear-shaped fruit used mostly as a vegetable. It ranges in color from ivory to light green. It's also known in other cultures as christophine and chayote.

**2 chochos (chayote) or cucumbers
2 whole scallions, finely sliced
1 egg, lightly beaten
2 tablespoons all-purpose flour
1 teaspoon baking powder
1 teaspoon salt
½ teaspoon ground white pepper
¼ cup cooking oil
¼ cup soy sauce**

Peel the chochos, slice them in half lengthwise and remove the pit. With a cheese grater, shred each half. In a bowl, combine the shredded chocho along with the scallions and egg. Add the flour, baking powder, salt and white pepper. Stir until all the ingredients are well combined.

Heat the oil in a large skillet until very hot. Place spoonfuls of the fritter batter into the skillet, frying until bubbles appear on top and the fritter is golden, about 1 minute. Flip the fritters and continue frying for 1 more minute until both sides are golden and the center is cooked. Blot off the oil with paper and serve the hot fritters with the soy sauce.

CODFISH FRITTERS
(STAMP AND GO)

MAKES 12 TO 16 FRITTERS (4 TO 6 SERVINGS)

Stamp and Go is up there with jerk pork as one of Jamaica's early fast foods. These fritters were a common roadside snack at the turn of the century. They make great spicy and crispy cocktail snacks that can be served with a chutney or cocktail sauce.

½ pound salt cod
1 cup all-purpose flour
1 cup coarse cornmeal
1 teaspoon baking powder
½ teaspoon salt
¼ teaspoon freshly ground black pepper
¼ cup plus 2 tablespoons vegetable oil
2 tablespoons minced onion
2 whole scallions, finely chopped
1 clove garlic, minced
¼ sweet green or red pepper, finely chopped
½ Scotch bonnet pepper (any color), seeded and minced
1 small tomato, finely chopped
½ teaspoon dried thyme
1 cup water (or more)

Soak the cod for 2 days in enough water to cover, changing the water each day. Steam it until cooked through, about 5 minutes. Flake and set it aside.

In a large bowl, combine the flour, cornmeal, baking powder, salt and black pepper.

Heat 2 tablespoons of the oil in a medium-size skillet and cook the onion, scallions, garlic, sweet pepper, Scotch bonnet pepper and tomato, stirring, for 2 minutes. Add the codfish and thyme to the pan and stir it to combine.

Add the cooked vegetables to the flour mixture and pour in the water, stirring until you have a slightly thick mixture which resembles pancake batter. (Add more water if it's too thick.)

Heat the remaining ¼ cup oil in a large skillet until it is very hot. Drop spoonfuls of the batter into the hot oil. Allow them to cook until bubbles form on the top, about 1½ minutes. Flip them over and continue to cook until the fritters are golden brown on both sides. Blot off the oil with paper and serve the fritters immediately with sauce.

NOTE These can be fried in advance and reheated in a 350°F oven for 10 minutes. Or you can microwave them for 1 minute.

SOLOMON GUNDY

**MAKES 1 QUART
(10 TO 12 SERVINGS)**

Serve this French-influenced fish spread on crackers with cocktails, but not if you want people to drink less; it's very salty.

3½ pounds pickled mackerel, herring and shad
    (proportions to taste)
¾ cup white vinegar
3 teaspoons ground allspice (dry pimento berries)
1 onion, minced
3 whole scallions, finely sliced
½ sweet green pepper, seeded and minced
1 tomato, chopped
1 Scotch bonnet pepper (any color), seeded and minced
½ teaspoon freshly ground black pepper
½ cup vegetable oil

Soak the fish in cold water for 2 hours. Drain and rinse it. Pour boiling water over it to loosen and remove the skin. Place the fish in a cooking pot, with enough water to cover, over high heat. Bring to a boil and cook for 5 minutes. Remove the fish from the pot and separate the flesh from the bones. Flake it into a bowl.

Combine the vinegar and allspice in a small cooking pot over high heat. Bring to a boil and cook for 2 minutes. Set aside. Add the onion, scallions, sweet green pepper, tomato, Scotch bonnet pepper, black pepper and oil to the bowl with the flaked fish. Mix together until well combined.

Remove the allspice from the vinegar and discard it. Pour the vinegar over the fish mixture and blend. Allow it to marinate for 1 day at room temperature. Store in covered jars in the refrigerator.

PLANTAIN FRITTERS

**MAKES 12 FRITTERS
(4 SERVINGS)**

Packed with potassium and lots of flavor, these simple cakes are great as an addition to any buffet or as a light snack. For a savory appetizer, sprinkle them with salt. Otherwise, use sugar for a sweet treat.

**2 ripe plantains
1 teaspoon baking powder
1 teaspoon salt or sugar
3 tablespoons cooking oil**

Wash the plantains and slice them in thirds, leaving the skins on. Place the pieces in a medium pan and cover with water. Bring to a boil over high heat and cook for 15 minutes or until the flesh is soft (test by inserting a knife).

Remove the plantains from the pan. Peel off the skins and mash the plantain to a smooth mush. You should have about 1 cup. In a small bowl, mix the mashed plantain with the baking powder and salt or sugar. Using your hands, form small cakes approximately 2½ inches in diameter. Heat the oil in a large skillet until it is very hot and fry the cakes over medium heat until golden, about 2 minutes per side.

CORNMEAL FRITTERS

MAKES 12 FRITTERS (6 SERVINGS)

These savory morsels complement many vegetarian entrees such as Quick-Fried Cabbage (page 39). The spice of the pepper combines with the sweetness of the coconut milk for a clean and complex, yet salt-free, flavor. Try them as appetizers topped with a spoonful of Pawpaw (page 104) or Mango Chutney (page 105).

**2 cups coarse or yellow cornmeal
1 teaspoon baking powder
2¼ cups coconut milk
1 onion, finely chopped
3 whole scallions, finely chopped
½ Scotch bonnet pepper (any color), seeded and
    minced, or ½ teaspoon hot sauce
½ cup vegetable oil**

In a medium-size bowl, mix together the cornmeal and baking powder. Add the coconut milk and stir until the batter is smooth. Add the onion, scallions and pepper, and stir the mixture until well combined. The batter should be moist yet firm enough to form into 2-inch patties with your hands. Add more cornmeal or liquid (coconut milk or water) if needed. (Rinse your hands with cold water before forming the patties so the batter doesn't stick to your hands.)

In a large skillet, heat the oil until it is very hot. Carefully place the patties into the skillet while lightly shaking the pan to keep them from sticking. Fry in batches until golden on both sides, about 3 minutes per side, using more oil if needed. Remove the fritters and drain them on paper. Serve while still hot.

NOTE These can be fried in advance and reheated in a 350°F oven for 10 minutes. Or you can microwave them for 1 minute.

BEEF PATTIES

**MAKES 18 PATTIES
(6 TO 9 SERVINGS;
2 PER PERSON
FOR LUNCH)**

The "hamburger" of Jamaica, a patty is the perfect snack or lunch. Layers of crispy dough enclose richly spiced meat. It is found on any corner in every town throughout the country. Prepared by few Jamaicans at home, patties are usually consumed on the run along with a box drink. Yet, they are simple and economical to prepare. Keep some uncooked in the freezer for a quick 15-minute bake-off. Also try the chicken, seafood and vegetarian versions.

FOR THE PASTRY
2½ cups all-purpose flour
½ teaspoon salt
¼ teaspoon baking powder
2 tablespoons curry powder
½ cup butter (1 stick)
½ cup margarine or lard (1 stick)
¾ cup ice-cold water

FOR THE FILLING
1 pound ground beef
1 onion, finely chopped
3 whole scallions, finely chopped
1 clove garlic, minced
2 Scotch bonnet peppers (any color), seeded and minced
1 teaspoon dried thyme or 2 sprigs fresh
¼ cup vegetable oil
2 teaspoons curry powder
1 teaspoon salt
½ teaspoon freshly ground black pepper
1½ to 2½ cups water
½ cup bread crumbs
1 egg, beaten with 1 teaspoon water

To make the pastry, combine the flour, salt, baking powder and curry powder in a large mixing bowl. Cut the butter and margarine into small pieces and add to the bowl. Working quickly and using your fingertips, squeeze together the flour mixture, butter and margarine and toss it together by scooping under the mixture with both hands. When the mixture resembles a very coarse meal, add the water to the bowl. With floured hands, mix and squeeze the dough just until it forms a ball. Knead it once or twice to combine it fully (the less kneading the better). Separate the dough into 2 pieces, flattening each into a thick pancake, wrap in plastic, and set them in the refrigerator to chill for at least 15 minutes.

(The dough will keep in the refrigerator up to 5 days. Remove it from the refrigerator 30 minutes before using it.)

For the filling, mix together the beef, onion, scallions, garlic, peppers and thyme in a large bowl. In a large skillet, heat the oil over high heat until it is very hot, and add the beef mixture. Fry until the meat is brown and the moisture is evaporated, about 8 minutes. Add the curry powder, salt and black pepper, stirring constantly over high heat, allowing a crust to form on the bottom of the pan.

Add the water and stir the mixture, scraping the bottom to incorporate the browned crust. Add the bread crumbs and stir. The consistency should be like a thick stew. Add more water as needed. Cover, reduce the heat to very low and cook for 15 minutes. Set it aside to cool.

Preheat the oven to 400°F. Cut each piece of the dough into 9 pieces. Using a rolling pin on a floured surface, roll out each piece of pastry into a rectangle shape with rounded edges. Spread a large spoonful of the cooled meat mixture over one side of the dough, leaving at least a ½-inch border on the outside edge. Using your finger, paint water around the border. Fold the other side of the dough over, and roll and crimp the edges. Lightly press a floured fork around the edge of the patty.

Place the patty onto a cookie sheet and repeat the procedure with the remaining dough. The patties may be covered in plastic and frozen at this point for later use. Brush each patty with the egg/water wash and bake for 20 minutes or until the patties begin to turn a golden color.

NOTE Serve as appetizers by making them miniature size.

VEGETABLE PATTIES

**MAKES 18 PATTIES
(6 TO 9 SERVINGS;
2 PER PERSON
FOR LUNCH)**

Vegetable patties are not the ubiquitous "patty" known to Jamaicans. But over recent years, they've become popular throughout Jamaica. The fillings vary greatly among cooks so be sure to use poetic license when creating your own.

A popular route between Ocho Rios and Kingston is Fern Gully (a four mile expanse of road that was originally a riverbed) where enormous walls of vegetation feature over six hundred species of the finest varieties of ferns, in all shapes and sizes. Along the journey is a roadside food stop known as Faith's Pen, a fast food "service station," Jamaican style. What started as a congregation of roadside huts has been organized by the government into a row of neat wooden structures with colorful signs announcing their names and specialties such as Ackee and Salt Fish and Jerk Chicken.

It is home to the often-mentioned Ragamuffin "Roots Tonic" juice bar, a fastidiously clean operation complete with fresh juice, sex tonics and a good collection of reggae dub music.

At Rose's Hot Spot, a Rastaman quietly and methodically prepares and cooks incredible vegetable patties. Hopefully, he'd approve of the following approximation, which bakes rather than fries the patties.

FOR THE PASTRY
2½ cups all-purpose flour
½ teaspoon salt
¼ teaspoon baking powder
2 tablespoons curry powder
½ cup butter (1 stick)
½ cup margarine or lard (1 stick)
¾ cup ice-cold water

FOR THE FILLING
1 tablespoon vegetable oil
2 cloves garlic, minced
1 small yellow onion, finely chopped
2 teaspoons curry powder
1 pound pumpkin, peeled and chopped (about 2½ cups)
1½ cups water
¼ head cabbage, shredded (about 1½ cups)
1 medium-size potato, diced
1 carrot, diced

½ chocho (chayote), peeled, pitted and diced (optional)
1 whole Scotch bonnet pepper (green recommended)
¾ teaspoon salt
½ teaspoon freshly ground black pepper
1 egg, beaten with 1 teaspoon water

To make the pastry, combine the flour, salt, baking powder and curry powder in a large mixing bowl. Cut the butter and margarine into small pieces and add to the bowl. Working quickly and using your fingertips, squeeze the flour mixture, butter and margarine together and toss it by scooping under the mixture with both hands. When the mixture resembles a very coarse meal, add the water to the bowl. With floured hands, mix and squeeze the dough just until it forms a ball. Knead it once or twice to combine it fully (the less kneading the better). Separate the dough into 2 pieces, flattening each into a thick pancake, wrap in plastic, and set them in the refrigerator to chill for at least 15 minutes. (The dough will keep in the refrigerator up to 5 days. Remove it from the refrigerator 30 minutes before using it.)

For the filling, heat the oil in a large skillet over medium heat. Add the garlic and onion, stirring constantly for 30 seconds. Add the curry powder and cook for 2 minutes, continuing to stir and scrape the bottom of the pan. (Do not burn!)

Add the pumpkin and ¾ cup of the water and blend it well with the curry mixture. Cover the skillet and reduce the heat to low. Simmer gently for 10 to 15 minutes or until the pumpkin is soft enough to mash.

Meanwhile, in a pot, add the cabbage and enough water to cover. Bring to a boil over high heat and cook for 3 minutes. Drain completely and set aside.

Crush the pumpkin until smooth, add the remaining ¾ cup water and stir. Add the cabbage, potato, carrot, chocho, Scotch bonnet pepper, salt and black pepper. Cover and simmer for 10 minutes. Remove the vegetable mixture from the skillet and place in a bowl. Let it cool. (It can be made ahead and will keep in the refrigerator, covered, for up to 5 days.) Remove the Scotch bonnet pepper before using.

Preheat the oven to 400°F. Cut each piece of the dough into 9 pieces. Using a rolling pin on a floured surface, roll out each piece of pastry into a rectangle shape with rounded edges. Spread a large spoonful of the cooled vegetable mixture over one side of the dough, leaving at least a ½-inch border on the outside edge. Using your finger, paint water around the border. Fold the other side of the dough over, and roll and crimp the edges. Lightly press a floured fork around the edge of the patty.

Place onto a cookie sheet and repeat the procedure with the remaining dough. The patties may be covered in plastic and frozen at this point for a later use. Brush each patty with the egg/water wash and bake for 20 minutes or until the patties begin to turn a golden color.

NOTE Serve as appetizers by making them miniature size.

CHICKEN PATTIES

**MAKES 6 TO 8
PATTIES
(4 TO 6 SERVINGS)**

Although similar in method to beef patties, these are often made in the shape of a bundle with the edges crimped on three sides over the top in a tent style.

One 3-pound chicken

FOR THE PASTRY
1¼ cups all-purpose flour
½ teaspoon salt
2 teaspoons curry powder
¼ cup margarine (½ stick)
2 tablespoons butter, chilled
3 tablespoons cold water

FOR THE FILLING
1 onion, chopped
3 whole scallions, finely sliced
1 clove garlic, minced
1 teaspoon fresh grated ginger or ½ teaspoon dried
    (optional)
1½ teaspoons dried thyme
1½ teaspoons salt
¼ teaspoon freshly ground black pepper
2 Scotch bonnet peppers (any color), seeded and minced
¼ cup vegetable oil
2 teaspoons curry powder
1 tomato, diced
½ cup plain bread crumbs
1½ cups water
1 egg, beaten with 1 teaspoon water

Rinse the chicken in cold water, place it in a large pot and cover it with water. Bring to a boil over high heat, then reduce the heat to low and simmer for 40 minutes.

Meanwhile, in a large mixing bowl, combine the flour, salt and curry powder. Cut the margarine and butter into small pieces and add to the bowl. Working quickly and using your fingertips, squeeze the flour mixture, margarine and butter together and toss by scooping under the mixture with both hands. When the mixture resembles a very coarse meal, add the water to the bowl. With floured hands, mix and squeeze the dough just until it forms a ball. Knead once or twice to form a ball (the less kneading the better). Separate the dough into 2 pieces, flattening each into a thick pancake, wrap in plastic, and chill for at least

15 minutes. (The dough will keep in the refrigerator up to 5 days. Remove it from the refrigerator 30 minutes before it is needed.)

Remove the chicken from the pot and cool. Remove the meat from the bone, shred it and set it aside. There should be about 2 cups.

Put the shredded meat into a mixing bowl along with the onion, scallions, garlic, ginger (if desired), thyme, salt, black pepper and Scotch bonnet pepper. Blend the mixture well and let it sit for at least 30 minutes at room temperature.

In a large skillet heat the oil over medium-high heat until it is hot. Add the curry powder and fry it for 1 minute. Add the chicken mixture and continue to cook, stirring, about 4 minutes. Add the tomato and stir, scraping the bottom of the pan, until the mixture is well blended and slightly dry. Mix in the bread crumbs. Slowly pour in the water until the consistency resembles a thick stew. Reduce the heat to low, cover and cook for 1 to 2 minutes. Transfer the mixture to a bowl and allow it to cool completely.

Preheat the oven to 400°F. Cut the dough into 6 pieces. Using a rolling pin on a floured surface, roll out each piece of pastry into a square shape with rounded edges. Spread a large spoonful of the cooled chicken mixture in the center of each piece. Using your fingertip, paint water around ½ inch of the outer edge. Pick up all 4 corners and crimp them together on top. Seal the 4 edges by gently pinching them together. Place the patties onto a cookie sheet. The patties may be frozen at this point for later use. Brush each patty with the egg/water wash and bake for 20 minutes or until the patties begin to turn a golden color.

NOTE Serve as appetizers by making them miniature size.

SHRIMP PATTIES

**MAKES 6 TO 8
PATTIES
(1 PER PERSON AS
THEY ARE SO RICH)**

This nouvelle alternative to the traditional Jamaican beef patty transforms it from a humble snack to an impressive offering. In Kingston, The Brick Oven Bakery sells a variety of such specialty patties. It's a popular lunch spot for locals and a worthwhile stop for travelers since it's located at Devon House, a national monument and museum, considered by many to be the finest example of Georgian architecture in Jamaica.

FOR THE PASTRY
1¼ cups all-purpose flour
½ teaspoon salt
1 teaspoon curry powder
¼ cup margarine (½ stick)
2 tablespoons butter, chilled
3 tablespoons cold water

FOR THE FILLING
3 tablespoons vegetable oil
1 small onion, finely chopped
2 whole scallions, finely sliced
2 teaspoons curry powder
1 tomato, diced
⅓ Scotch bonnet pepper (any color), seeded and minced
2 sprigs fresh thyme or ¾ teaspoon dried
½ teaspoon salt
¼ teaspoon freshly ground black pepper
½ cup sliced okra
½ pound medium shrimp, peeled, deveined and sliced
⅓ cup water
1 egg, beaten with 1 teaspoon water

For the pastry, combine the flour, salt and curry powder in a large mixing bowl. Cut the margarine and butter into small pieces and add it to the bowl. Working quickly and using your fingertips, squeeze the flour mixture, margarine and butter together and toss it by scooping under the mixture with both hands. When the mixture resembles a very coarse meal, add the water to the bowl. With floured hands, mix and squeeze the dough just until it forms a ball. Knead it once or twice to combine it fully (the less kneading the better). Separate the dough into 2 pieces, flattening each into a thick pancake, wrap in plastic, and set them in the refrigerator to chill for at least 15 minutes. (The dough will keep in the refrigerator up to 5 days. Remove it from the refrigerator 30 minutes before it is needed.)

In a large skillet, heat the oil over medium-high heat until it is very hot. Add the onion and scallions and cook, stirring, for 1 minute. Add the curry powder and continue cooking for 1 minute. Add the tomato, Scotch bonnet pepper, thyme, salt and black pepper and cook, stirring, for 2 minutes. Add the okra, shrimp and water to the pan. Stir to combine, and continue cooking until the shrimp is just cooked, about 3 minutes. Remove the thyme sprigs. Put the shrimp mixture into a small bowl and refrigerate until completely cool.

Preheat the oven to 400°F. Cut the dough into 6 pieces. Using a rolling pin on a floured surface, roll out each piece of pastry into a rectangle shape with rounded edges. Spread a large spoonful of the cooled shrimp mixture over one side of the dough, leaving at least a ½-inch border along the outside edge. Using your finger, paint water around the border. Fold the other side over, and roll and crimp the edges. Lightly press a floured fork around the edge of the patty. Place it onto a cookie sheet and repeat the procedure with the remaining dough. The patties may be frozen at this point for later use. Brush each patty with the egg/water wash and bake them for 20 minutes or until the patties begin to turn a golden color.

NOTE Serve as appetizers by making them miniature size.

TURNED CORNMEAL

MAKES 6 SERVINGS (PLUS 2 EXTRA FOR MORNING-AFTER LEFTOVERS)

This versatile preparation is similar to Italian polenta. It can be eaten on its own, or it pairs nicely with any well-sauced dish such as Brown Stew Fish (page 78). If you're lucky enough to have leftovers, slice and fry it as a tasty side for your morning eggs.

2 tablespoons vegetable oil
1 onion, finely chopped (about 1 cup)
3 whole scallions, finely sliced
1 tomato, chopped (about ½ cup)
¼ sweet green or red pepper, seeded and chopped
3 okra, sliced (about ¼ cup) (optional)
4 cups coconut milk
2 cups coarse cornmeal
1 teaspoon salt
½ teaspoon freshly ground black pepper
¼ Scotch bonnet pepper (any color), seeded and minced
¼ teaspoon dried thyme

In a medium-size skillet, heat the oil over medium-high heat until it is very hot. Add the onion, scallions, tomato, sweet pepper and okra. Cook, stirring until well blended and slightly dry, about 2 minutes. Remove from the heat.

In a thick-bottomed saucepan, heat the coconut milk over low heat. Add the cornmeal, cooked vegetables, salt, black pepper, Scotch bonnet pepper and thyme. Cook for 20 minutes, turning frequently with a large, strong utensil.

If serving immediately, spoon the cornmeal directly onto the plates. Otherwise, place the mixture in a serving dish and form it into a mold. When you are ready to serve, cut it into wedges.

A simpler version of this recipe from a Jamaican friend goes like this: Fry an onion with a likkle wata and trow in de kahnmeal of 1 pownd. Turn and turn adding wata, 1 pint and a likkle.

CORN BREAD

MAKES 6 TO 8 SERVINGS

The only grain in this corn bread recipe is cornmeal, making it suitable for the many folks who are wheat intolerant and for those of us who enjoy the simplest, truest formula. Otherwise, you can substitute some wheat flour for part of the cornmeal, achieving a lighter-textured bread.

**2 cups coarse cornmeal or 1½ cups cornmeal plus ½ cup
    wheat flour
2½ teaspoons baking powder
½ teaspoon salt
1¼ cups coconut milk or other milk
2 eggs
¼ cup butter or margarine, melted (½ stick)**

Preheat the oven to 400°F. Lightly grease an 8-inch-square cake pan and set it aside. In a large bowl or the bowl of a mixer, combine the cornmeal, baking powder and salt. In a separate small bowl, combine the milk and eggs and beat them with a fork or whisk. Add it to the dry mixture along with the butter or margarine and stir until it is well blended. Pour into the greased cake pan and bake for 25 minutes.

VARIATION
Experiment by folding other things into the batter, such as shredded coconut, diced red pepper or cooked corn kernels.

BREAD STUFFING

MAKES 3 CUPS

A roast chicken meal is so much more exciting with stuffing. It fills you up and tastes great. This stuffing can also be stuffed into chochos for a nice side dish.

6 to 8 slices bread (any kind)
3 tablespoons butter or margarine
2 onions, chopped
3 stalks celery, chopped
½ teaspoon dried thyme
1 teaspoon salt
½ teaspoon freshly ground black pepper
¼ to ½ cup water or chicken broth

Crumble the slices of bread in a blender or food processor. You should have about 2 cups. Spread the crumbs on a large plate and allow them to dry out a little.

In a skillet over medium-high heat, melt the butter or margarine. Add the onions and celery and cook, stirring, until they begin to soften, about 3 minutes. Add the bread crumbs, thyme, salt and black pepper. Stir until the mixture is well combined. Add enough water to make a proper stuffing consistency.

NOTE Corn Bread crumbs from the previous page can replace bread crumbs in this recipe.

FESTIVAL

MAKES 8 SERVINGS

Festival is a relative newcomer to Jamaican cooking. Not until about fifteen years ago did it begin to pop up at Hellshire Beach, where local vendors sell it with fried fish. It's similar to a Johnny Cake except for its shape and slightly sweet flavor. It is one of the few additional menu offerings along with jerk at the Boston Beach jerk pits and other larger jerk centers. The crispy sweetened cornmeal is a great foil for the spicy jerk meat.

1 cup all-purpose flour
¾ cup coarse cornmeal
2 tablespoons sugar
½ teaspoon salt
1 teaspoon baking powder
⅛ teaspoon ground allspice (dry pimento berries)
1 teaspoon vanilla
¾ cup milk
2 cups vegetable oil

In a large bowl, mix together the flour, cornmeal, sugar, salt, baking powder and allspice. In another bowl, combine the vanilla and milk. Slowly stir the milk mixture into the flour mixture to achieve a thick batter. Turn the batter onto a floured surface, knead the dough lightly and form it into a log shape. Divide it into 8 pieces. With floured hands, roll each piece into a 4-inch-long sausage shape.

Heat the oil in a large, deep skillet over high heat until it is very hot. Fry the dough, turning each piece until golden brown all over, 5 to 6 minutes. Drain on paper towels before serving.

SAVORY SNACKS AND SIDES

19

JOHNNY CAKES

MAKES 6 TO 8 JOHNNY CAKES (4 TO 6 SERVINGS)

Eaten with a traditional breakfast such as ackee and salt fish, these cakes, originally called "Journey Cakes," are served with meat and seafood on many Caribbean islands.

2 cups all-purpose flour
2 teaspoons baking powder
½ teaspoon salt
2 tablespoons butter
¼ cup water, approximately
1 cup vegetable oil

In a large bowl, sift together the flour, baking powder and salt. Using your fingertips, rub in the butter. Add just enough water to achieve a stiff, smooth dough. Shape the cakes into 2-inch-wide discs.

Heat the oil in a large skillet over high heat until it is very hot. Fry the cakes in the hot oil until they are brown on both sides, 5 to 7 minutes.

DUMPLINGS

**FLOUR DUMPLINGS
MAKES 6 ROUND
"FOOD" DUMPLINGS
OR ENOUGH
SPINNERS FOR
1 POT OF SOUP**

**CORNMEAL
DUMPLINGS
MAKES EIGHT
2-INCH ROUND
DUMPLINGS
(ENOUGH FOR
1 POT OF SOUP)**

Jamaicans take their dumplings very seriously! There are "spinners," small oblong ones that are served in soups and stews. Larger round dumplings are boiled and served as "food" alongside a main dish. Fufu is a type of dumpling made of any starch food, such as green banana, yam, corn or cassava, and served in stews or as a dish by the same name. Johnny Cakes are a fried version of a dumpling.

Some cooks use baking soda to lighten the dumpling and others don't. Once again, it's up to your personal preference, so the recipe here is just a basic guideline.

There are no cooking directions for these two dumpling recipes because more specific instructions are provided elsewhere. They are called for in other recipes throughout the book, such as Red Pea Soup on page 34, Pumpkin Soup on page 31, and Beef Soup on page 24.

FLOUR DUMPLINGS
1 cup all-purpose flour
¼ teaspoon salt
⅓ cup water

In a medium-size bowl, combine the flour and salt. Stir in the water to distribute it evenly into the flour. With your hands, knead it to form a soft and smooth dough.

CORNMEAL DUMPLINGS
1 cup coarse cornmeal
¼ cup all-purpose flour
½ teaspoon salt
½ cup water, approximately

In a medium-size bowl, combine the cornmeal, flour and salt. Stir in the water (adding more or less as needed) to distribute evenly into the cornmeal-flour mixture. With your hands, knead it to form a soft and smooth dough.

SOUPS

BEEF SOUP

**MAKES 10
HEARTY SERVINGS**

Traditionally served as Saturday lunch, this soup is filled to the brim with vegetables and spinners (oblong dumplings). The simple name belies its complete ability as a truly nutritious one-pot meal. It's even better as a leftover and freezes nicely. You may add or subtract types of vegetables or amounts depending on their availability. Just follow the basic plan, adding the softer vegetables with the spinners.

1 salted pig's tail (optional)
3 pounds beef with bone, such as short ribs or shin
1 pound pumpkin, peeled and cubed
1 large onion, chopped
1 large turnip, chopped
2 carrots, sliced
$\frac{1}{4}$ cup fresh minced parsley
16 cups water
2 chochos (chayote), peeled, pitted and chopped or
    2 cucumbers, peeled, seeded and chopped
2 medium-size potatoes, peeled and chopped
1 pound yam (white or yellow), peeled and chopped
1 whole Scotch bonnet pepper plus 2 slices (any color),
    or other hot chili pepper
1 tablespoon salt, or to taste

FOR THE SPINNERS
1 cup all-purpose flour
$\frac{1}{4}$ teaspoon salt
$\frac{1}{3}$ cup water

If you are using the pig's tail, soak it in 2 separate water baths for 10 minutes each and rinse after each soaking.

Place the pig's tail and the beef bones in a large soup pot (an oval Dutch oven is ideal). Add the pumpkin, onion, turnip, carrots, parsley and water. Bring to a boil over high heat, then reduce the heat and simmer partially covered for about $1\frac{1}{2}$ hours or until the beef is tender.

Meanwhile, place the chochos, potatoes and yam in a large bowl of cold water and set aside.

To prepare the spinners, in a medium-size bowl, sift together the flour and salt. Stir in the water to distribute evenly into the flour mixture. With your hands, knead the mixture to form a soft and smooth dough. Cover and set aside.

When the beef is tender, add to the pot the chochos, potatoes, yam, whole Scotch bonnet pepper and pepper slices. Form the spinners by rolling small pieces of dough between your floured palms to form 1-inch oblong shapes, and drop them into the soup one at a time. Stir gently to prevent the spinners from sticking to the bottom. Continue to cook for 15 minutes or until the potatoes are tender but not mushy. Remove the pig's tail and the whole Scotch bonnet pepper from the pot. If desired, remove the beef bones: Separate the beef from the bone, cut the beef into small pieces, and return it to the soup, discarding the bones. Taste for salt and add more as needed. (You will need at least 1 tablespoon if the salted pig's tail was not used.)

OXTAIL SOUP

MAKES 6 TO 8 SERVINGS

The oxtail makes a rich and intensely flavored soup. Any beef lover will appreciate it.

½ pound oxtail
⅓ cup large dry white beans (lima or broad)
10 cups water
½ yam, peeled and chopped (about ½ pound)
1 chocho (chayote), peeled, pitted and chopped,
    or 1 cucumber, peeled, seeded and chopped
1 tomato, chopped
2 whole scallions, sliced
1 clove garlic, minced
1 sprig fresh thyme or 1 teaspoon dried
2 teaspoons salt
½ teaspoon freshly ground black pepper
1 whole Scotch bonnet pepper (any color)

FOR THE SPINNERS
1¼ cups all-purpose flour
¼ teaspoon salt
½ cup water

Wash the oxtail in water and place it in a large soup pot along with the beans and water. Bring to a boil over high heat, then reduce the heat to medium-low and simmer, partially covered, for 2 hours. Add the yam, chocho, tomato, scallions, garlic, thyme, salt, black pepper and Scotch bonnet pepper. Simmer for 45 minutes more.

For the spinners, combine the flour, salt and water. Knead the dough until you have a smooth, sticky ball. With 20 minutes left of cooking time, add the spinners one at a time to the soup. Roll a small piece between the palms of your hands, forming a narrow, oval shape, and drop into the soup. Simmer for 20 minutes. Remove the Scotch bonnet pepper before serving.

BROAD BEANS SOUP

MAKES 6 SERVINGS

Broad beans, also called butter beans, are similar to lima beans and are used fresh or dried. Often found stewed with oxtail or tripe, they make a terrific alternative to the commonly used red peas (kidney beans).

¾ **pound dried broad beans**
8 **cups water**
½ **pound beef with bones, such as short ribs or shin**
2 **cloves garlic, sliced**
1 **teaspoon salt**
¾ **teaspoon sweet paprika**
2 **sprigs fresh thyme or 1½ teaspoons dried**
½ **teaspoon freshly ground black pepper**
1 **pound yellow yam**
3 **chochos, peeled, pitted and chopped, or 3 cucumbers, peeled, seeded and chopped**
2 **carrots, peeled and chopped**

FOR THE SPINNERS
1¼ **cups all-purpose flour**
¼ **teaspoon salt**
½ **cup water**

Rinse the beans and soak them in water to cover overnight. In a large soup pot, place the drained beans and the water. Bring to a boil and add the beef bones and garlic. Reduce the heat to a brisk simmer and cook for 30 minutes, covered.

Skim off the froth and continue cooking for 1½ hours or until the beans are tender.

Meanwhile, prepare the dumplings. In a medium-size bowl, sift together the flour and salt. Add the water and blend with a wooden spoon until a ball is formed. Flour your hands and knead slightly to form a soft dough. Add more flour if the dough is too sticky. Cover and set aside.

Remove ½ cup of the beans, mash them in a separate bowl and return them to the pot.

Add the salt, paprika, thyme and black pepper. Continue cooking while peeling and chopping the yam. Add the yam along with the chochos and carrots.

Form the spinners by rolling small pieces of dough between your floured palms to form 1-inch oblong shapes and drop them into the soup one at a time. Stir gently to prevent the spinners from sticking to the bottom. Cook an additional 15 to 20 minutes or until the vegetables are tender.

CHICKEN SOUP

MAKES 6 TO 8
LARGE SERVINGS

Nowadays, many Jamaicans use a packaged chicken soup called cock soup as a base for various soups. To me, it tastes artificial and seems to replace all the natural goodness of real chicken. Jamaica has delicious chickens that make great homemade soup! Also known as "Jewish penicillin," chicken soup has been prescribed since the twelfth century as a bronchial cure. It's an even more potent brew with onions, garlic and lots of chili pepper. Here's an old-fashioned recipe, Jamaican style.

3 pounds chicken parts with bones
2 onions, chopped
3 cloves garlic, minced
1 pound pumpkin, peeled and chopped
2 white turnips, peeled and chopped
3 carrots, chopped
3 cabbage leaves, shredded (about ½ cup)
1 chocho (chayote), peeled, pitted and chopped or 1
**   cucumber, peeled, seeded and chopped**
10 cups water
1½ teaspoons salt
½ teaspoon freshly ground black pepper
1 whole Scotch bonnet pepper (any color)
½ cup cooked noodles

Rinse the chicken thoroughly and place in a large soup pot along with the onions, garlic, pumpkin, turnips, carrots, cabbage, chocho and water. Bring to a boil, then reduce the heat to medium-low and simmer uncovered for 40 minutes. Add the salt, black pepper and Scotch bonnet pepper and continue to cook for 20 to 30 minutes or until the chicken is tender. Turn off the heat. Remove the chicken from the pot and refrigerate until it is cool enough to handle.

Remove the chicken meat from the bone and discard the bones and skin. Shred the chicken meat and add it to the soup pot along with the cooked noodles. Heat completely before serving piping hot.

For a reduced fat soup, refrigerate the soup for at least 3 hours and skim the coagulated fat from the surface before reheating and serving.

NOTE Don't hesitate to add or subtract vegetables depending on availability or your taste.

VARIATION
Cooked rice can replace the noodles.

CONCH SOUP

MAKES 4 TO 6 SERVINGS

Conch soup or chowder turns up periodically on a Jamaican menu, but one would expect to see it more often given the abundance of shells on display for tourists. Cooked properly, conch meat has a nice chewy texture and a subtle seafood flavor.

1 pound conch
Juice of 2 limes
2 quarts water
1 chocho (chayote), peeled, pitted and chopped or
    1 cucumber, peeled, seeded and chopped
1 potato, peeled and chopped
1 tomato, diced
1 onion, chopped
1 sprig fresh thyme or 1 teaspoon dried
½ teaspoon salt
¼ teaspoon freshly ground black pepper
1 whole Scotch bonnet pepper plus 2 slices (any color)

Wash the conch in batches of water until the water comes out clean. Drain and cut it into small pieces. Place in a bowl and pour in the lime juice. Mix around to fully coat the meat. Remove the conch from the lime juice and place it in a medium saucepan along with the 2 quarts of water, and boil it for 1½ hours. Add the chocho, potato, tomato, onion, thyme, salt, black pepper, and whole and sliced Scotch bonnet pepper. Bring to a boil again, then reduce heat to medium-low and simmer for 40 minutes. Remove the whole Scotch bonnet pepper. Serve immediately.

FISH TEA

The word "tea" is often used in Jamaica to describe different types of hot beverages, no doubt due to the British influence on the local language.

You'll find fish tea in seaside places where items like steamed or roasted fish are served. Depending on the local fish, the soup differs slightly from region to region. The dense-fleshed turbot used on the south coast makes for a much creamier texture, while up north, snapper and parrot fish produce a lighter and thinner broth.

2 pounds fish with head and bones
2 green bananas or Irish potatoes, chopped
½ pound pumpkin, peeled and diced
**1 chocho (chayote), peeled, pitted and chopped or 1
    cucumber, peeled, seeded and chopped**
1 potato, peeled and chopped
¼ pound okra, sliced
3 whole scallions
1 teaspoon dried thyme
1 whole Scotch bonnet pepper (any color)
½ teaspoon salt
½ teaspoon freshly ground black pepper
10 cups water

Place all of the ingredients in a large soup pot and bring to a boil over high heat. Reduce the heat to medium-low and simmer for 1 hour. Remove the Scotch bonnet pepper. Strain out the fish bones, if desired, before serving.

GREEN BANANA SOUP

MAKES 6 TO 8 SERVINGS

The green banana is a staple in most of the West Indian countries. In Jamaica, it's a common side dish or "food," served with just about any main dish. This soup has a subtle flavor and creamy texture from the cooked green bananas. It tastes even better on the second day.

1 pound beef with bones, such as short ribs or shin
2 whole scallions, crushed
1 carrot
1 stalk celery
8 cups water
6 green bananas or Irish potatoes, chopped
4 tomatoes, chopped
2 whole scallions, sliced
2 cloves garlic, minced
½ teaspoon dried thyme
2 teaspoons salt
¼ teaspoon freshly ground black pepper
1 whole Scotch bonnet pepper (green recommended)
1 cup coconut milk
2 potatoes, peeled and chopped
¼ pound yellow yam, peeled and chopped

Rinse the beef and place it in a large soup pot along with the crushed scallions, carrot, celery and water. Bring to a boil, cover, reduce the heat to medium-low and simmer for 1 hour.

Meanwhile, cut the bananas in half and score the peel down to the flesh along the vertical lines. Place in a pot of boiling water and boil for 2 minutes. Drain the bananas and put them in cold water for about 15 seconds. Peel, dice and set them aside.

When the beef stock is done, drain it and discard the vegetables. Separate the meat from the bones and chop the meat into small pieces.

Return the stock to the pot and add the tomatoes, sliced scallions, garlic, thyme, salt, black pepper, Scotch bonnet pepper, coconut milk, potatoes, yam, diced green bananas and chopped beef.

Stir well and bring it to a boil. Cover, reduce the heat to medium-low and simmer for 30 minutes.

PUMPKIN SOUP

**MAKES 6 TO 8
SERVINGS**

*My fondest childhood memory of Jamaican food is pumpkin soup.
Spinners (small, elongated dumplings) swimming in the nourish-
ing orange broth make this simple soup a treasure trove. Yellow or
white yams can be used instead of or in addition to spinners.
Unfortunately, many Jamaicans now opt for packaged seasoning
over bones and the slow-simmering soup pot. What a shame! Serve
as a light meal or as a dinner starter.*

½ **pound pig's tail, salted (optional)**
3 **pounds beef with bone, such as short ribs or shin**
2 **pounds pumpkin, peeled and cubed**
10 **cups water**
3 **whole scallions, crushed**
2 **cloves garlic, crushed**
1 **whole Scotch bonnet pepper plus 2 slices (any color)**
1 **sprig fresh thyme or 1 teaspoon dried**
1½ **teaspoons salt (optional)**
½ **teaspoon freshly ground black pepper**
½ **pound yellow or white yam, peeled and chopped
     (optional)**

FOR THE SPINNERS
1¼ **cups all-purpose flour**
¼ **teaspoon salt**
½ **cup water**

If you are using a pig's tail, soak it in two 10-minute water baths and rinse. Place
it in a large soup pot along with the beef, pumpkin and water. Bring to a boil,
reduce the heat to medium-low and simmer until the pumpkin has dissolved and
the beef is tender, about 1½ hours.

Meanwhile, to prepare the spinners, in a medium-size bowl, sift together the
flour and salt. Add the water and blend with a wooden spoon until a ball is formed.
Flour your hands and knead slightly to form a soft dough. Add more flour if the
dough is too sticky. Cover and set aside.

When the meat is tender, remove it from the pot. Separate the meat from the
bones, chop it and return it to the pot. Bring to a brisk simmer over medium heat
and add the scallions, garlic, Scotch bonnet pepper, thyme, salt (if not using pig's
tail) and black pepper. If using, place the yam in the pot.

Bring to a simmer again. Form the spinners by rolling small pieces of dough
between your floured palms to form 1-inch-long oblong shapes. Drop the spinners into the soup one at a time. Stir gently to prevent them from sticking to the
bottom. Continue to cook the soup for 15 minutes. Remove the Scotch bonnet
pepper before serving.

PEPPERPOT SOUP

MAKES 6 TO 8 SERVINGS

This soup is dominated by the mineral-rich leafy green known as callaloo, which is similar to spinach. It has its origin with the Arawak Indians, who were the first known inhabitants of Jamaica. Over the years it's evolved from a callaloo-based stew to more of a soup dish using a vast array of vegetables. Different recipes derive their rich flavor bases from either smoked pork, shrimp, crab or salt cod, depending on the availability of ingredients or taste preference.

½ pound callaloo or spinach, chopped
½ pound kale, chopped
½ pound smoked pork, such as ham hocks
½ pound beef with bones, such as shin
10 okra, chopped
1 tomato, chopped
1 whole Scotch bonnet pepper (green recommended)
10 cups water
5 whole scallions, chopped
3 cloves garlic, minced
2 sprigs fresh thyme or 1½ teaspoons dried
2 teaspoons salt
¾ teaspoon freshly ground black pepper
1 to 4 slices Scotch bonnet pepper (any color)
1 chocho (chayote), peeled, pitted and chopped or
    1 cucumber, peeled and chopped
½ pound yellow yam, peeled and chopped (optional)
2 cups fresh or canned coconut milk

FOR THE DUMPLINGS
1¼ cups all-purpose flour
½ teaspoon salt
⅓ cup water

Wash the callaloo or spinach and kale thoroughly by submerging in 2 to 3 different cold water baths. Lift the greens out first, then discard the water. Place the greens in a large soup pot (a Dutch oven is ideal) along with the pork, beef, okra, tomato, whole Scotch bonnet pepper and water. Bring to a boil, reduce the heat to medium-low and partially cover. Simmer for 1½ hours.

Remove the whole Scotch bonnet pepper. Take out the pork and beef from the pot and separate the meat from the bone and fat. Chop the meat and return it to the pot. Add the scallions, garlic, thyme, salt, black pepper, sliced Scotch bonnet pepper, chocho, yam and coconut milk. Cook for 30 minutes, adding water if needed for a proper soup consistency.

To prepare the dumplings, in a medium bowl, sift together the flour and salt. Add the water and blend with a wooden spoon until a ball is formed. Flour your hands and knead slightly to form a soft dough. Form it into flat round shapes (will make 8 to 10). Cook them in boiling water for 15 minutes. Serve the soup piping hot with a dumpling in each bowl.

NOTE Don't hesitate to use other vegetables, such as pumpkin, sweet pepper, cabbage or Irish potatoes, as replacements or additions if you have any on hand.

RED PEA SOUP

**MAKES 6 TO 8
SERVINGS**

Red peas are what folks outside Jamaica know as kidney beans. This is one of the most popular soups in Jamaica and it's certainly economical. It varies from cook to cook but has the same basic elements in common, often distinguished by a smoked meat. This is a hearty soup, suitable as a complete meal in itself, yet it also makes a nice starter for a large meal. You may make substitutions for the recommended vegetables, yams for potatoes, etc. Vegetarians may omit the ham hock and beef.

1 pound dried red peas (kidney beans)
2 pounds soup beef with bones
1 ham hock or other smoked pork
11 cups water
1 carrot, finely chopped
1 chocho (chayote), peeled, pitted and chopped or
    1 cucumber, peeled, seeded and chopped
1 Irish potato, peeled and chopped
1 whole Scotch bonnet pepper (green recommended)
2 slices Scotch bonnet pepper (any color)
3 cloves garlic
3 whole scallions
1 sprig fresh thyme or 1 teaspoon dried
2 teaspoons salt
½ teaspoon freshly ground black pepper

FOR THE SPINNERS
1¼ cups all-purpose flour
¼ teaspoon salt
½ cup water

Rinse the red peas, beef and ham hocks separately and place them in a large soup pot with 10 cups of the water. Bring to a boil over high heat. Reduce the heat to medium-low and partially cover the pot. Cook at a brisk simmer until the peas are soft and the meat is tender, about 2 hours.

Meanwhile, to prepare the spinners, in a medium-size bowl, sift together the flour and salt. Add the water and blend with a wooden spoon until a ball is formed. Flour your hands and knead slightly to form a soft dough. Add more flour if it is too sticky. Cover and set aside.

Remove the beef and pork from the pan and set aside. With the back of a spoon, mash some of the peas in the soup pot.

Add the carrot, chocho, potato, whole and sliced Scotch bonnet peppers, garlic, scallions, thyme, salt, black pepper and remaining cup of water. Cook for 30 minutes longer. With 15 minutes of cooking time left, form the spinners by rolling small pieces of dough between your floured palms to form 1-inch-long oblong shapes. Drop into the soup one at a time. Stir gently to prevent the spinners from sticking to the bottom.

Remove the meat from the bones of the beef and pork. Discard the bones, chop the meat into small pieces and return it to the soup pot. Remove the whole Scotch bonnet pepper, scallions and thyme sprig (if using). Serve immediately or refrigerate it until needed. Blend in 1 cup more water if you are reheating it.

VARIATION

For an even heartier soup, drop in spinners with 20 minutes cooking time left. If you are reheating the soup, be careful that the spinners don't stick to the bottom of the pan.

VEGETABLES, BEANS AND RICE

AVOCADO SALAD

MAKES 6 SERVINGS

The avocado, or "pear" as it's known in Jamaica, has been eaten since 1492 when Christopher Columbus came to the Caribbean. It's been called "poor man's butter" and today remains a favorite vegetable, most often just served peeled and sliced as a side to the morning meal or with a sweet snack.

3 cups shredded lettuce
3 ripe avocados
Juice of 1 lime
1 teaspoon salt
1 small onion, finely sliced
2 small tomatoes, quartered
½ teaspoon ground white pepper or black pepper

Spread out the lettuce on a platter. Peel and slice the avocado, discarding the pit, and place it in a bowl. Toss the avocado slices with the lime juice and salt. Arrange the pieces evenly over the lettuce. Place the onion and tomatoes over the top. Sprinkle the pepper on top.

STUFFED AVOCADO

**MAKES 2 SERVINGS
AS A SIDE DISH**

In this preparation, I like to use low-fat yogurt, but mayonnaise or sour cream is also fine.

1 ripe avocado
½ lime
3 tablespoons plain low-fat yogurt
1 tomato, chopped
1 whole scallion, finely chopped
1 tablespoon chopped parsley
¼ teaspoon salt
¼ teaspoon freshly ground black pepper

Halve the avocado and remove and discard the pit. Squeeze the lime over both sides. In a bowl, mix together the yogurt, tomato, scallion, parsley, salt and black pepper. Heap the filling into each side of the avocado and serve. It will keep in the refrigerator for 1 hour before serving.

QUICK-FRIED CABBAGE

MAKES 6 SERVINGS

Serve this alongside Cornmeal Fritters (page 7) and fresh Limeade (page 110) or Fresh Mint Tea (page 115) for a light vegetarian lunch or supper. The small tender cabbage found in Jamaica bear little resemblance to our large sturdy variety, but the flavor combination is still delicate and satisfying. This is an all-time favorite cabbage dish.

1 medium-size head cabbage (about 3 pounds)
¼ cup vegetable oil
1 small onion, thinly sliced (1 cup)
1 scallion, sliced
½ sweet green or red pepper, chopped
1 tomato, chopped (about ½ cup)
2 sprigs fresh thyme or 1½ teaspoons dried
1 teaspoon salt (optional)
1 whole Scotch bonnet pepper (any color)

Peel off the tough outer leaves of the cabbage and remove the inner core. Shred what remains and set it aside.

Heat the oil in a large skillet over medium-high heat until hot. Add the onion, scallions, sweet pepper and tomato. Raise the heat to high and cook until the vegetables have softened, about 5 minutes. Stir in the thyme, salt and Scotch bonnet pepper. Add all of the cabbage to the pan and stir to combine it with the onion mixture. Cover and reduce the heat to medium-low. Cook for 10 minutes, stirring occasionally. The recipe can be prepared in advance to this stage.

Remove the cover and continue to cook until the cabbage is tender but not too soft, about 5 minutes. Remove the hot pepper and thyme sprigs before serving.

VARIATION

This dish can also be prepared with carrots, which will make it sweeter and even more wholesome and colorful. Add ½ to 1 cup of shredded carrots to the skillet with the cabbage.

CALLALOO

This abundant, leafy green has a firmer texture and fuller flavor (not bitter) than spinach. It is the main ingredient in Pepperpot Soup (page 32) and can be found in callaloo loaf at patty shops. Mineral-rich callaloo is another staple vegetable in every Jamaican's diet.

**2 pounds callaloo (see Note)
1 tablespoon cooking oil
1 tablespoon butter
1 onion, chopped
3 whole scallions, chopped
1 sprig fresh thyme or ½ teaspoon dried
½ teaspoon salt
½ teaspoon freshly ground black pepper
⅓ cup water**

Remove the small branches with leaves from the main stem and submerge the callaloo into a bowl of cold water. Let soak for a minute and remove, discarding the water. Repeat 2 more times. Finely chop the leaves and branches and set aside.

Heat the oil and butter in a medium-size skillet over medium heat until the butter is melted. Add the onion and scallions, stirring until the onion begins to soften, about 2 minutes. Add the callaloo, thyme, salt and black pepper. Mix all of the ingredients together, add the water and cover. Cook over medium heat until the stems are tender, about 8 minutes.

NOTE Swiss chard or mustard greens are suitable substitutes for this dish. Spinach can become too mushy.

CELERY AND RICE

MAKES 6 TO 8 SERVINGS

Straight out of the Ital tradition, salt-free and scented with a hint of fresh ginger, this refreshing combination rounds out any vegetarian meal.

2 tablespoons vegetable oil
3 to 4 stalks celery, chopped (about 2 cups)
1 tablespoon chopped onion
1 tablespoon fresh minced ginger
1½ cups uncooked long-grain white rice
1 slice Scotch bonnet pepper, any color (optional)
2¼ cups water

Heat the oil in a medium-size saucepan with a tight-fitting lid over medium-high heat. Add the celery, onion and ginger and cook, stirring, until the mixture begins to soften, about 2 minutes. Add the rice and stir to blend. Add the Scotch bonnet pepper and pour in the water. Raise the heat to high and bring to a boil. Cover, reduce the heat to medium-low and simmer for 20 minutes.

CHOCHOS AND CUCUMBERS

MAKES 4 TO 6 SERVINGS

These two vegetables, with similar textures and the ability to absorb other flavors, combine to form an alliance whose sum is greater than its parts. Combined with green peppers, they have a lovely green color, which complements any main dish.

3 onions, chopped
2 chochos (chayote), peeled, pitted and chopped
2 cucumbers, peeled, seeded and chopped
1 green pepper, thinly sliced lengthwise
3 tablespoons vegetable oil
1 teaspoon salt

In a bowl, combine the onions, chochos, cucumbers and green pepper.

Heat the oil in a large skillet over high heat. Add the vegetables and salt and cook, stirring, until the onions soften and the chocho and cucumbers just begin to sweat, 2 to 3 minutes. Serve hot or cold.

STUFFED AND
BAKED CHOCHOS

**MAKES 4 SERVINGS
OR 8 AS A SIDE DISH**

The pear shape of chocho makes it ideal for stuffing. The naturally subtle-tasting flesh, which is similar to cucumber, works well with a variety of other foods as it absorbs any flavor into its own. Don't hesitate to experiment with your own stuffing. These make a great lunch, light supper or side dish with a larger meal.

4 chochos (chayote) or cucumbers
½ pound ground beef
1 small onion, finely chopped
1 clove garlic, minced
½ Scotch bonnet pepper (any color), seeded and minced
½ teaspoon dried thyme
1 tablespoon oil
1 tablespoon butter
¼ cup plain bread crumbs (preferably fresh)
¾ cup grated white cheddar cheese
½ teaspoon Worcestershire sauce
½ teaspoon salt
¼ teaspoon freshly ground black pepper

In a large pot of boiling water, cook the chochos until they are tender, about 20 minutes. Meanwhile, in a large bowl, combine the beef, onion, garlic, Scotch bonnet pepper and thyme. Refrigerate until needed.

Remove the chochos from the boiling water and set aside. When they are cool enough to handle, cut each one in half and remove the pits. Scoop out some of the flesh from each half by scoring it first with a small, sharp knife and then lifting it out with the edge of a spoon. Be sure to leave enough flesh around the skins to keep them sturdy. Dice the flesh and put it aside in a small bowl. Preheat the oven to 400°F.

In a large skillet, heat the oil and butter until very hot. Add the meat mixture and cook until browned, 8 to 10 minutes. (Clean the bowl and set it aside.) Add the diced chocho to the pan and cook it for 2 minutes. Return the meat and chocho mixture to the bowl. Add the bread crumbs, ½ cup of the cheese, Worcestershire sauce, salt and black pepper and mix well.

Spoon a large scoop of filling into each chocho half. Place pieces next to each other in a large ovenproof pan. Put any leftover stuffing into a small ovenproof baking dish. Sprinkle the remaining ¼ cup of cheese on each chocho half. Bake for 10 to 15 minutes.

VARIATIONS

For a vegetarian version of this dish, substitute 1 cup cooked brown rice for the meat. Cucumbers can be used in place of chochos. Rinse them well and halve them lengthwise. Complete as directed, except boil them for 5 to 10 minutes instead of 20.

MIXED GREENS

MAKES 6 SERVINGS

A nice alternative to callaloo is a mélange of mixed greens. These nutritional powerhouses and their cruciferous cousins are loaded with important minerals, such as calcium and iron, which are proven cancer fighters. Just contrast color and texture, choosing from the many greens available today, like spinach, mustard, chard, dandelion or beet, and mix with something from the cabbage family.

1 pound spinach or other tender, leafy green
1 pound cabbage or kale
2 tablespoons vegetable oil
1 onion, sliced
½ Scotch bonnet pepper (any color), seeded and minced
1 tablespoon white vinegar
½ teaspoon salt
½ teaspoon freshly ground black pepper

Rinse the greens thoroughly in 3 baths of water (there's nothing worse than grit!). With some water still clinging on, shred the greens and cabbage and put them in separate bowls.

Heat the oil in a large skillet over medium-high heat and add the onion and Scotch bonnet pepper. Cook, stirring, for 2 minutes. Add the cabbage and mix it together, cooking for 2 minutes more. Add the spinach, stirring as it wilts and mixes with the cabbage. Add the vinegar, reduce the heat to medium-low, cover and simmer for 5 minutes. Stir in the salt and black pepper.

COLE SLAW

MAKES 8 TO 10 SERVINGS

Slaw is a common vegetable garnish in Jamaica made with tender young cabbage. It is a fresh and healthy salad that is often served without dressing.

1 cabbage, shredded
2 to 3 carrots
2 tomatoes, seeded and diced
1 cucumber, peeled, seeded and diced
½ green pepper, seeded and diced
½ cup yogurt
½ cup mayonnaise
2 tablespoons honey
2 tablespoons cane or apple cider vinegar
1 teaspoon salt
½ teaspoon freshly ground black pepper

First, place the cabbage in a large bowl, then blend in the carrots. Fold in the tomatoes, cucumbers and green pepper. Cover and refrigerate until ready to serve.

Combine the yogurt and mayonnaise in a small bowl. Mix in the honey, vinegar, salt and black pepper. Adjust the seasonings to taste and refrigerate.

Just before serving, slowly add the dressing to the vegetable mixture, stirring and adding just enough until desired creaminess is achieved.

BOILED GREEN BANANAS

MAKES 4 TO 6 SERVINGS

This is only for the Jamaican cooking initiates who might not be familiar with the green banana. Since it is served as a side dish with so many dishes, it's important to know how to cook it.

6 green bananas

Wash the bananas and cut both ends off each one. Make slices through the skin along all of the vertical lines on the banana. Place in a pot and cover with water. Boil for 10 minutes. Peel the bananas and serve.

SPICED CORN ON THE COB

MAKES 6 TO 8 SERVINGS

Try this as an alternative to roast corn, which is best fresh out of the field. This transforms any old corn by cooking it for a long time and adding lots of spices.

6 to 8 ears of corn, shucked
1 tablespoon salt
1 tablespoon freshly ground black pepper
1 whole Scotch bonnet pepper (any color) or 1 teaspoon hot sauce
3 tablespoons butter
4 cloves garlic

Cut each shucked ear of corn into 2-inch pieces and place in a pot just large enough to fit the corn snugly. Add enough water to cover the corn.

Add the salt, black pepper, Scotch bonnet pepper, butter and garlic. Bring to a boil over high heat, cover and reduce the heat to medium-low. Simmer for 30 minutes. Check periodically to assure the water level remains the same. Add more water as needed. Rotate the corn in the pot for even cooking.

FRIED PLANTAIN

The Spanish introduced plantains to Jamaica in the sixteenth century, and they are a widely used starch throughout the Spanish-speaking West Indies as well.

For this preparation, use very ripe plantains (the skins should be completely black). It's served as a side dish along with or instead of dumplings or green bananas and is a must for Sunday lunch.

3 very ripe plantains
3 tablespoons vegetable oil
2 tablespoons butter

Cut off both ends of the plantains and slice through the skin lengthwise into 3 pieces. Cut these into ¼-inch diagonal slices.

Heat the oil and butter in a large skillet over high heat until they are bubbling but not smoking. Shake the pan slightly as you place each piece of plantain in the hot fat. Fry each piece on one side until it becomes a dark golden color, about 2 minutes. Turn each piece and repeat. Remove the pieces to a paper towel. Drain and serve immediately.

NOTE The plantains may be fried in advance and reheated in a 325°F oven for 10 minutes.

PLANTAIN CAKES

MAKES 12 CAKES (6 SERVINGS)

This popular side dish or snack is a great alternative to the usual plantain preparations. Mineral rich and highly nutritious, plantains are also quite filling. A boon in ethnic cooking has given foods such as plantains a wider availability, so it is hoped more and more people will become familiar with this multidimensional vegetable. On the American table, try them as an alternative to sweet potatoes for the Thanksgiving feast.

3 very ripe plantains
½ teaspoon baking powder
1 tablespoon light or dark brown sugar
½ teaspoon vanilla
Juice of ½ orange
½ teaspoon grated orange rind
¼ cup vegetable oil

Wash the plantains and cut off the ends. Slice them through their skins along the vertical lines. Place them in a large saucepan and cover completely with water. Bring to a boil over high heat and cook until tender, about 15 minutes.

Remove the cooked plantains from the pan and peel. In a large bowl, mash the flesh to a soft, lumpy consistency. Add the baking powder, brown sugar, vanilla, orange juice and rind. Mix until well combined.

Heat the oil in a large skillet over medium-high heat until it is very hot. Rinsing your hands in cold water first, pat out small thin cakes the size of silver dollars. Place the cakes in the hot oil and cook until browned on both sides, about 4 minutes per side. Drain on paper towels and serve.

NOTE Use your taste to guide you, adding shredded coconut or cinnamon for a different flavor.

VARIATION

For a fat-free version that is good for a buffet table, double the recipe and bake, rather than fry, the batter in a square pan for 15 minutes at 350°F. Cut into squares before serving.

PUMPKIN VEGETABLE CURRY STEW

MAKES 6 SERVINGS

This stew is an excellent vegetarian main dish, and the pumpkin gives you a large dose of beta-carotene for a boost to the immune system. Serve it with Rice and Peas (page 49) and chutney.

3 tablespoons vegetable oil
1 onion, finely chopped
2 cloves garlic, minced
2 tablespoons curry powder
½ teaspoon cinnamon
½ teaspoon ground ginger
1 teaspoon salt (optional)
½ teaspoon freshly ground black pepper
2 tomatoes, chopped
⅔ cup water
1 pound pumpkin, peeled and chopped
1 carrot, sliced
1 potato, chopped
1 green banana or Irish potato, chopped
1 whole Scotch bonnet pepper (green recommended)

Heat the oil in a large skillet over medium-high heat. Add the onion and cook, stirring, for 2 minutes. Add the garlic and cook 1 minute longer. Add the curry powder, cinnamon, ginger, salt and black pepper and cook, stirring, for 2 minutes. Add the tomatoes and stir until it is a thick, relishlike sauce.

Add the water, scraping the bottom of the pan to incorporate all the flavors. Add the pumpkin, carrot, potato, green banana and Scotch bonnet pepper. Raise the heat to high and bring to a boil while gently blending the ingredients together. Cover, reduce the heat to medium-low and simmer, stirring a couple of times, until the vegetables are tender, about 20 minutes. Remove the Scotch bonnet pepper before serving.

RICE AND PEAS

MAKES 6 SERVINGS

Every Jamaican household, rich or poor, serves this nutritionally complete one-pot meal. It's the backbone of this island's cuisine, hence its moniker, "Jamaica Coat of Arms." Along with fried plantains, it's a Sunday lunch staple, yet for my money it's a perfect choice all by itself for any meal any day. This basic recipe has many variations according to personal tradition. I prefer not to use Scotch bonnet pepper, keeping it as a sweet, smooth complement to the robustly spiced dishes.

½ **pound dried red peas (kidney beans) or small red
    beans (1 cup)**
6 to 8 cups coconut milk
1 teaspoon freshly ground black pepper
2 whole scallions, crushed
2 sprigs fresh thyme or 1½ teaspoons dried
2 cups uncooked long-grain white rice
2 teaspoons salt

Wash the beans thoroughly and place them in a medium-size saucepan with the coconut milk, black pepper, scallions and thyme. Bring to a boil over high heat, then reduce the heat to low, cover and simmer for 1 to 2 hours or until the beans are almost tender (adding water as needed to keep the beans covered). Remove the thyme (if using whole sprigs) and scallions. Add the rice and salt. If necessary, add more water so that the liquid is 1 inch above the rice. Bring it to a boil over high heat, then reduce the heat, cover and simmer for 20 minutes. Fluff it with a fork. The grains of rice should easily separate and not be mushy.

STEW PEAS AND RICE

This tasty dish is a frugal way to use up those chicken necks and backs leftover from so many chicken recipes. Any beef or pork you might have on hand will also give the beans a deep, rich flavor.

2 to 3 pounds chicken, beef or pork
1 onion, sliced
1 teaspoon salt
½ teaspoon freshly ground black pepper
1½ teaspoons dried thyme
⅜ to ½ pound red peas (kidney beans)
6 cups water

FOR THE RICE
2 cups uncooked long-grain white rice
3 cups water
1 teaspoon salt

Rinse the meat and pat it dry with a paper towel. Place it into a bowl and combine with the onion, salt, black pepper and thyme. Allow to season for 1 hour in the refrigerator. Place the meat and red peas in a large pot with the water and bring to a boil over high heat. Reduce the heat and simmer for 1 to 2 hours or until the red peas have reached the desired consistency. Add more water if needed.

Meanwhile prepare the rice. Combine the rice, water and salt in a medium-size saucepan with a tight-fitting lid. Bring it to a rolling boil, cover and reduce the heat to the lowest setting. Cook for 20 minutes. Serve the beans spooned over the rice.

VARIATION
Replace the red peas with broad beans.

BAKED
SWEET POTATOES

**MAKES 6 TO 8
SERVINGS**

Glazed with a sweetened lime-rum topping, this is the perfect side dish for roast chicken or pork.

**2 pounds sweet potatoes, washed
1 teaspoon grated orange rind
¼ teaspoon ground nutmeg
½ teaspoon salt
¼ teaspoon ground white pepper
½ cup light or dark brown sugar
2 tablespoons butter
1 tablespoon fresh lime juice
3 tablespoons dark rum**

Preheat the oven to 400°F. Bake the sweet potatoes for 1 hour. Remove from the oven and reduce the heat to 350°F. When cool enough to handle, peel and slice the potatoes. In a medium-size baking dish, arrange the slices in layers, sprinkling the orange rind, nutmeg, salt and white pepper over each slice.

In a small pan over medium-low heat, heat the brown sugar, butter, lime juice and rum until the sugar is dissolved. Pour this mixture over the top of the layered sweet potatoes and bake until the glaze is golden, about 40 minutes. Cool slightly before serving.

TOMATO-ONION STEW

MAKES 6 SERVINGS   *For this soft, relishlike complement to crispy Fried Chicken (page 61), I thank, once again, the incomparable Miss Lamita Freeburn of Darliston in the Parish of Westmoreland.*

3 tablespoons vegetable oil
4 onions, thinly sliced
1 clove garlic, minced
5 tomatoes, cut in eighths lengthwise
1 teaspoon salt
½ teaspoon freshly ground black pepper

Heat the oil in a medium-size skillet over medium-high heat. Add the onions and cook, stirring, for 3 minutes. Add the garlic and cook 2 minutes more. Add the tomatoes and cook 5 minutes more. Add the salt and black pepper and stir. Serve hot or cold.

VARIATION
One thinly sliced green pepper can be added along with the onions.

VEGETABLE SALAD

MAKES 6 SERVINGS

This salad is found in different styles on many tables throughout Jamaica. It's the freshness of the vegetables and the way they are cut and laid out that makes it worthy of explanation. Serve it with Rice and Peas (page 49) for a light, enjoyable meal.

1 small head leafy green lettuce, separated, washed
     and dried
3 to 4 carrots, peeled and shredded
2 sweet green peppers, thinly sliced lengthwise
2 mild onions, thinly sliced
¼ cup vinegar
½ teaspoon prepared mustard
½ clove garlic, minced
¼ teaspoon salt
⅛ teaspoon freshly ground black pepper
¾ cup olive oil

On a large serving platter, arrange the lettuce leaves to cover the entire surface. In the center, place a pile of shredded carrots next to a pile of sliced green pepper. Layer the sliced onion all around the edge.

Place the vinegar, mustard, garlic, salt, black pepper and olive oil into a jar with a tight-fitting lid. Shake until well incorporated. Serve the dressing on the side along with the salad.

STRING BEAN AND
CARROT MEDLEY

MAKES 6 SERVINGS   *This combination is often found in a simple vegetable side dish as a part of a larger meal. The care local farmers in Jamaica take in using the rich soil yields vegetables with the most profound flavors. The green and orange color is also a pleasing sight on the plate.*

1 pound string beans
4 carrots
2 tablespoons butter
1 teaspoon salt
½ teaspoon freshly ground black pepper

Wash and remove the ends from the beans and slice them diagonally into 1-inch pieces. Peel the carrots and slice them into thin discs. Toss the two vegetables together and place them in a steamer or a pot with ½ inch of water. Cover and cook gently until just tender, 4 to 5 minutes.

In a bowl, toss the vegetables with the butter, salt and black pepper, and turn them onto a large serving plate.

RICE

WHITE RICE
MAKES 6 TO 8
SERVINGS

BROWN RICE
MAKES 6 TO 8
SERVINGS

Since rice is commonly served with so many Jamaican dishes, here is my foolproof recipe. The ratio is 1 part rice to 1½ parts water for white rice.

More and more folks are appreciating the health benefits of brown rice. It takes more time than white rice but is well worth the wait. Leftover brown rice makes an excellent ground beef substitute.

WHITE RICE
2 cups uncooked long-grain white rice
3 cups water
1 teaspoon salt

Combine the rice, water and salt in a medium-size saucepan with a tight-fitting lid. To avoid starchy rice, be careful not to stir excessively. Bring to a rolling boil, cover and reduce heat to the lowest setting. Cook for 22 minutes.

BROWN RICE
2 cups uncooked short- or long-grain brown rice
3¼ cups water
1 teaspoon salt

Combine the rice, water and salt in a medium-size saucepan with a tight-fitting lid. To avoid starchy rice, be careful not to stir excessively. Bring to a rolling boil, cover and reduce the heat to the lowest setting. Cook for 1 hour.

POULTRY AND MEAT

CHICKEN FRICASSEE

MAKES 6 TO 8 SERVINGS

This delicious and popular dish is intuitively prepared in several variations by Jamaicans. Don't confuse the rustic Jamaican style with the French, cream-based sauce. A few simple ingredients and a quick preparation result in a most unusual taste and a satisfying meal. Serve with white rice, Fried Plantain (page 46) and Cole Slaw (page 44) or Avocado Salad (page 38).

Two 3-pound chickens
2 limes, rinsed and quartered
1 teaspoon salt
½ teaspoon freshly ground black pepper
4 small yellow onions, thinly sliced
4 tomatoes, chopped
4 cloves garlic, minced
1 sprig fresh thyme or 1 teaspoon dried
1 whole Scotch bonnet pepper (green recommended)
1 to 3 slices Scotch bonnet pepper (red recommended)
¼ cup vegetable oil
2 cups water or chicken stock

Rinse the chickens and pat them dry with a towel. Cut the chickens into serving pieces. To make a quick stock, if desired, place the chicken backs, necks and wing tips into a small pot and cover with water. Bring to a boil, reduce the heat to low and simmer until needed.

Place the other chicken pieces in a large bowl and squeeze the limes over them, coating each piece with juice. (Leave the lime rinds in the bowl.) Sprinkle on the salt and black pepper, add the onions, tomatoes, garlic, thyme and Scotch bonnet peppers, and mix well. Set aside to marinate for at least 15 minutes.

In a large skillet, heat half of the oil over high heat until it is very hot. Fry half the pieces of chicken until golden on both sides, about 5 minutes per side. Remove the pieces from the pan and set aside on a large plate. Wipe out the old oil and add the remaining oil. Repeat the frying process with the rest of the chicken pieces. Remove the chicken from the pan and pour out the oil. Discard the lime rinds from the tomato mixture. Return the pan to medium-high heat, add all the chicken pieces and tomato mixture and cook, stirring, for 3 minutes. Blend in the water or chicken stock. Reduce the heat to medium-low, cover and simmer until the chicken is tender, 40 to 45 minutes. Remove the whole Scotch bonnet pepper. Serve the chicken with the sauce spooned over it.

CHICKEN AND RICE

MAKES 6 SERVINGS

This preparation takes its influence from the Spanish dish Arroz con Pollo, *which simply combines the chicken and rice in one pot for cooking. It can feed a crowd economically and is a perennial favorite.*

One 3- to 4-pound chicken
1 teaspoon salt
¼ teaspoon freshly ground black pepper
1 teaspoon dried thyme
3 tomatoes, peeled and seeded
1 onion, roughly chopped
2 cloves garlic
¼ cup vegetable oil
2 cups uncooked long-grain white rice

Rinse the chicken thoroughly and pat it dry with a towel. Cut the bird into serving pieces. Put the backbone, neck and wing tips in a pot with enough water to cover. Bring to a boil, reduce the heat to low, and leave simmering until the chicken broth is required.

Sprinkle the salt, black pepper and thyme over the chicken parts and set aside. Place the tomatoes, onion, garlic and ½ cup of the simmering chicken broth in a blender jar and process until smooth.

Heat the oil in a large skillet over medium-high heat until it is very hot. Add the chicken parts and cook, covered, until golden on both sides, about 4 minutes. Reduce the heat to medium and add the rice, stirring and scraping the bottom of the pan until the rice begins to turn a light golden color.

Add the tomato mixture and blend until well combined. Simmer briskly for 2 minutes. Add 2½ cups of the simmering stock, supplementing with water if needed. Cover and reduce the heat to low. Cook for 30 minutes, turning the chicken over after 15 minutes. Serve hot or reheat in a 325°F oven for 20 minutes.

VARIATIONS

Boneless chicken can be used. Reduce the final cooking time to 20 minutes. Water may be substituted for the chicken broth.

CHICKEN AND PEANUT (GROUNDNUT) STEW

MAKES 4 TO 6 SERVINGS

The use of peanuts in Jamaican cooking comes from the West African tradition. Most Jamaicans are familiar with the word pinda *from a line in a children's game, "Pop-si kai-si go pinda shell." Pinda is another word for peanut, which comes from* mpinda, *meaning "ground-nut, peanut" in the African Kikongo language.*

With the African slaves came their particular dietary habits. The geography of West Africa would have been similar enough to that of Jamaica to have provided them with the same type of foods as those they were accustomed to back home in Africa—from peanuts to yam, corn and pumpkin.

Groundnut stew has several variations depending on the addition of certain vegetables. Serve it with Turned Cornmeal (page 16) and Mixed Greens (page 43).

One 3- to 4-pound chicken
1 small onion, peeled, plus 1 cup chopped onion
1-inch piece of fresh ginger
2½ cups water
2 tablespoons vegetable oil
¾ cup tomato sauce
⅔ cup peanut butter
2 teaspoons salt
1 teaspoon cayenne pepper or ½ Scotch bonnet pepper (any color), seeded and minced

Rinse the chicken and cut it into 8 pieces. Reserve the back, neck and wing tips for stock or another use. Boil the chicken, whole onion, ginger and water in a large pot for 15 minutes.

Meanwhile, heat the oil in a large skillet over medium-high heat until it is very hot. Cook the chopped onion, stirring, until golden, about 3 minutes. Add the tomato sauce and cook 3 minutes more. Blend in the peanut butter, salt and cayenne pepper.

Turn off the heat under the chicken pot, remove the chicken parts and drain out the broth from the chicken pot, blending it into the tomato–peanut butter mixture.

Add the chicken parts to the skillet and cover. Reduce the heat and simmer until the chicken is tender, 15 to 20 minutes. This dish can be prepared in advance to this stage and gently reheated with a little water.

NOTE This is a fairly spicy dish that can be altered to taste by reducing the amount of cayenne pepper.

VARIATIONS

Carrots, yams, sweet potatoes or regular potatoes can be added together along with the broth. Add an additional cup of water. Or, instead, add chopped eggplant and okra.

FRIED CHICKEN

MAKES 6 TO 8 SERVINGS

One of the best fried chicken recipes I've encountered anywhere comes from Miss Lamie, the cook from Woodstock Farm in the peaceful Parish of Westmoreland. Serve it with her Tomato-Onion Stew (page 52), boiled potatoes and a fresh vegetable salad for a proper Lamie-style feast!

Two 3- to 4-pound chickens
2 teaspoons salt
1½ teaspoons freshly ground black pepper
2 teaspoons dried thyme
2 onions, sliced
3 cups plain bread crumbs (preferably fresh)
2 eggs
½ cup vegetable oil

Rinse the chickens well in cold water and pat them dry with paper towels. Cut each chicken into 8 pieces, reserving the neck, back and wing tips for stock or another use. Place the chicken pieces in a large bowl and combine with the salt, pepper, thyme and onions. Leave it to season refrigerated for 1 hour.

Spread out the bread crumbs on a plate. In a small bowl, beat the eggs together and pour them over the chicken, coating each piece completely. Roll each chicken piece in the bread crumbs.

If possible, heat equal parts of the oil in 2 large skillets over high heat until very hot. (Otherwise do it in 2 batches.) Place half of the chicken in each skillet and brown it on both sides, about 40 minutes, turning it once halfway through the cooking time. Remove the chicken to a plate covered with paper towels to drain off the oil. Serve immediately.

NOTE This chicken is excellent cold and is a perfect choice for a picnic.

CURRY CHICKEN

MAKES 6 TO 8 SERVINGS

Chicken became the meat of choice for the English in their curry dishes, although the East Indians, who brought the style with them, used goat. Today, curry is an essential flavor and preparation style in Jamaican cooking. Commercial curry powder varies greatly in quality and flavor. It loses its punch if allowed to sit in the cupboard too long. For purists, making the powder from fresh spices is the best. Serve this with white rice and chutney. This dish is even better the next day. Hopefully there will be leftovers.

Two 3-pound chickens
2 limes
½ cup vegetable oil
2 tablespoons butter (optional)
3 small onions, chopped
5 cloves garlic, minced
5 tablespoons curry powder
3 tomatoes, chopped, or ¼ cup tomato sauce
1 Scotch bonnet pepper (any color), plus 2 to 4 slices
    (any color)
2 teaspoons salt
¾ teaspoon freshly ground black pepper
4 cups water

Rinse the chickens with water and pat them dry with paper towels. Cut the chickens into serving pieces and place into a large bowl, reserving the backs, necks and wing tips for stock or another use. Juice the limes and add the juice to the chicken along with the grated lime rind, coating the chicken with the juice.

In a large skillet, heat ¼ cup of the oil and 1 tablespoon of the butter, if using, over high heat until very hot. Pat the chicken dry again and carefully add half of the pieces to the skillet. Fry on one side for 3 minutes, shaking and tilting the skillet a little to distribute the fat. Turn the chicken over and fry for 3 minutes more or until golden brown. Remove the chicken to a large platter and set aside.

Pour out the old fat, wipe the skillet and add the remaining ¼ cup oil and 1 tablespoon butter, if using. Repeat the frying procedure with the remaining chicken pieces and then set aside.

Discard all but 2 tablespoons of oil, reduce the heat to medium and add the onions and garlic to the skillet. Cook, stirring, for 1 minute (be careful not to burn the garlic). Add the curry powder and fry for 1 more minute, scraping the bottom.

Add the tomatoes, whole Scotch bonnet pepper and slices, salt and black pepper. Stir thoroughly while scraping the bottom of the pan. Add the water and mix until well blended. Return the chicken to the pan. Bring it to a boil and reduce the heat to a simmer. Cover and cook for 45 minutes or until the chicken is tender.

VARIATION
Add ½ cup of shredded coconut just before serving.

GINGER STEWED CHICKEN

MAKES 4 TO 6 SERVINGS

With Jamaica having arguably the best ginger on the planet, ginger features prominently in all areas of cooking and folk remedies. This recipe is adapted from a clipping out of the Daily Gleaner, *one of Jamaica's newspapers. It uses a lot of fresh, pulverized ginger, which completely permeates the chicken. Serve it with white rice and Mixed Greens (page 43).*

One 3- to 4-pound chicken
Juice of 1 lime
1 teaspoon salt
¼ teaspoon ground white pepper
¼ to ½ pound fresh ginger, peeled and pulverized
¼ cup vegetable oil
2¼ cups water
1 teaspoon all-purpose flour
2 teaspoons Worcestershire sauce
1 onion, thinly sliced
Salt to taste

Rinse the chicken, pat it dry with paper towels, and rub it with the lime juice. Cut the chicken into serving pieces, reserving the back, neck and wing tips for stock or another use. Sprinkle on the salt and white pepper. Rub the pulverized ginger on each piece of the chicken.

Heat the oil in a medium-size skillet over high heat until it is very hot. Add the chicken pieces and cook until lightly golden brown, about 4 minutes per side. Add 2 cups of the water to cover the chicken. Bring to a boil, then cover and reduce the heat to medium-low. Simmer for 20 minutes. Turn over the chicken pieces and continue to simmer briskly, uncovered, for 20 more minutes. Meanwhile, combine the flour, Worcestershire sauce and remaining ¼ cup of water and set aside.

Remove the chicken from the pan and stir in the flour mixture. Add the onion and simmer for 5 minutes. Add salt to taste. Return the chicken to the pan and coat it in sauce. This can be made in advance and reheated.

JERK

This is a backyard version of a Jamaican barbecue that was originally practiced by the tenacious Maroons of Jamaica to preserve the meat of wild hogs. Maroons are descendants of slaves of the Spanish and British who escaped into the rugged mountainous interior known as the Cockpit country. They fought tirelessly for independence from the British. In 1739, peace treaties granted them land and the right to self-government. Eventually it was not uncommon to see a Maroon man selling jerked pork at island markets. Jerk evolved into a type of barbecue preparation that uses salt, pepper and pimento to smoke domestic pork, chicken and fish.

Today jerk is eaten at roadside barbecues in practically every corner of the island. Makeshift grills billowing with smoke are a common sight along any road.

Boston Bay Beach in the Parish of Portland is considered the current jerk mecca, although many a jerk man challenges that notion with his own "special version." Jerk's unique flavor is derived primarily from the pimento tree. Its wood is used for smoking, its young green branches for grill stands *(patas)* and its berries (known to most as allspice) are crushed into a sauce for seasoning along with scallions, salt and Scotch bonnet pepper. Recipes vary and optional ingredients include cinnamon, ginger, nutmeg, soy sauce, black pepper and onion, to name a few.

JERK CHICKEN

MAKES 6 TO 8

For takeout at a roadside jerk stand, this slow-cooked fast food servings comes cleverly wrapped and placed in a white rectangle cardboard cake (charlotte) box. Spoon on some hot sauce, clamp down the lid, grab a napkin and you're ready to roll. Chop the meat before serving, bone and all, since half the fun is picking through the rubble for the prized meat. To serve the most proper guests, boned chicken thighs are quicker and easier. Serve as a light meal with Festival (page 19), Johnny Cakes (page 20) or hard dough bread.

5 bunches whole scallions, finely chopped
3 large cloves garlic, minced
3 Scotch bonnet peppers (any color), seeded and minced
2 sprigs fresh thyme or 2 tablespoons dried
¼ cup ground allspice (dry pimento berries)
2 tablespoons freshly ground black pepper
1½ tablespoons salt
1 cup water
5 pounds chicken thighs or 2 small whole
**   chickens cut into quarters (see Note)**

Combine all ingredients except the water and chicken in a large bowl. Mix well and add the water to form a loose paste.

Reserve ½ cup of the sauce for a later use. Marinate the chicken in the remaining sauce for at least 1 hour or as long as 24 hours (the longer the better). Turn the meat several times, mixing the sauce.

Prepare an outdoor barbecue using plenty of coals. Meanwhile, soak small sticks or hardwood chips in water (mesquite conflicts with jerk's own flavor). When the coals have become gray and well ashed over, add the soaked wood to the fire.

Place the chicken on the grill and cover, leaving the vent holes open. Barbecue *slowly*—1½ to 2 hours, depending on the size of the pieces. Check the fire after 30 minutes, adding coal or wood as needed and being careful not to flame the fire. Baste every 30 minutes with the marinade. Turn the chicken several times as it cooks. The chicken is done when it is firm to the touch and slightly charred.

Remove the chicken from the fire and let it sit on a cutting board for 15 minutes. If you have a sharp cleaver, chop the meat into small pieces (bone and all); otherwise, leave each piece whole. Serve on a large platter doused with the reserved jerk sauce.

NOTE For boneless chicken thighs (breasts tend to dry out), use the same preparation, but change the barbecue time to 30 or 40 minutes. Cut into large bite-size pieces.

ORANGE GINGER CHICKEN

**MAKES 4 TO 6
SERVINGS**

Chinese Jamaicans are one of the many rich cultural groups that have contributed to the tapestry of Jamaican cooking. Chinese food is very popular in present-day Jamaica and several good Chinese restaurants thrive.

The Chinese first came to Jamaica as indentured servants after the abolition of slavery, and the Chinese influence in present-day Jamaica is pervasive. Their cooking methods and flavor combinations have crept into Jamaican cooking as seen in many sweet-and-sour preparations. This recipe draws from this flavor tradition. Serve it along with lots of fluffy white rice.

One 3- to 4-pound chicken
1 onion, chopped
1 whole scallion, chopped
1 clove garlic, minced
½ Scotch bonnet pepper (any color), seeded and minced
½ teaspoon ground allspice (dry pimento berries)
½ teaspoon salt
⅛ teaspoon freshly ground black pepper
Juice of 2 oranges
¼ cup soy sauce
2 tablespoons ginger marmalade or orange marmalade
**   plus 1 teaspoon fresh grated ginger**
⅓ cup vegetable oil
½ cup water or chicken stock
2 tablespoons cornstarch

Cut the chicken into pieces and rinse thoroughly with water. Pat the pieces dry with paper towels and place them in a large bowl. Add the onion, scallion, garlic, Scotch bonnet pepper, allspice, salt and black pepper. Put aside to season for 30 minutes.

In a small bowl, combine and mix the orange juice, soy sauce and ginger marmalade.

Heat the oil in a large skillet over high heat until it is very hot. Add the chicken (reserving the seasoning) and brown it until golden, about 10 minutes. Remove the chicken from the pan and set aside. Pour out most of the oil. Add the leftover meat seasoning to the pan and cook over medium heat for 3 minutes, stirring constantly. Add the water or stock and return the chicken to the pan. Raise the heat, bring to a boil, and then cover and reduce the heat to low. Simmer for 20 minutes.

Meanwhile, blend the cornstarch with a small amount of the orange mixture, forming a smooth paste, and add the remaining orange mixture, stirring until well blended. Stir this into the pan over medium heat and cook for 20 more minutes. The sauce will thicken. Serve immediately or reheat with a little water.

VARIATION

Boneless chicken may be used instead of chicken parts. Slice the meat into thin slices and reduce the cooking time from 20 minutes to 10 minutes .

ROAST CHICKEN

Always a popular favorite, roast chicken is ideal for a meal, a picnic, a sandwich or a snack. Jamaican seasoning combinations can be prepared in many different ways, but the trick is getting the whole bird browned outside while keeping the flesh tender and juicy. Serve it with Mixed Greens (page 43) and Corn Bread (page 17).

Two 3½-pound chickens or 1 large roaster
1 onion, roughly chopped
1 whole scallion, chopped
2 cloves garlic
1 tomato, chopped
1 teaspoon dried thyme
1 teaspoon salt
½ teaspoon freshly ground black pepper
1 tablespoon soy sauce
1 teaspoon Worcestershire sauce
1 tablespoon vegetable oil
Juice of ½ lime
1 to 2 tablespoons water

Rinse the chickens thoroughly with water and pat them dry with paper towels. Prick the skin all over with a fork and place the chickens in a large bowl.

Put all the other ingredients into a food processor or blender jar and process until it resembles a thick relish. Add more water if needed.

Rub the sauce all over the cavities and outside of the chickens. Cover and let it marinate refrigerated for at least 30 minutes and up to 5 hours.

Preheat the oven to 425°F. Put the chickens on a rack in a roasting pan or on a cookie sheet, breast side down. Roast the chickens for 30 minutes, then reduce the heat to 350°F and turn the birds over so they are breast side up. Pour any remaining marinade over them. Roast them for 45 minutes, then return the heat to 425°F for the final 15 minutes, or until they are a deep golden brown all over. (Total cooking time is 1½ hours.)

Let the chickens sit, outside of the oven, 10 to 15 minutes before carving.

VARIATION

The birds can be stuffed with Bread Stuffing (page 18). Increase the cooking time at 350°F by 10 minutes.

BEEF STEW

MAKES 6 TO 8 SERVINGS

One of my favorite dishes and a classic dish in many cultures is beef stew, also known as stewed beef. Jamaicans might serve theirs with steamed rice and boiled green bananas. This is an easy recipe that requires minimal ingredients. This nonspicy version is friendly for everyone. But don't forget to have a fiery bottle of hot sauce on the table.

4 pounds stew beef without bones, such as chuck, well trimmed and cubed
1½ teaspoons salt
¼ teaspoon freshly ground black pepper
¼ cup vegetable oil
1 tablespoon butter (optional)
2 small onions, chopped
1 clove garlic, minced
½ sweet red pepper, seeded and finely chopped
1 tomato, chopped
2½ cups water
2 potatoes, cubed
3 carrots, sliced

Place the beef into a large bowl. Season it with ½ teaspoon of the salt and the black pepper. In a large skillet over high, heat the oil until it is very hot. (Keep a lid nearby for splattering oil.)

Carefully place some of the meat into the pan without crowding it. Fry for 4 minutes on each side to achieve a golden brown crust. Remove from the pan with a slotted or webbed spoon. Repeat the procedure with the remaining beef. Turn the heat down to low. (The pan should have a dark brown, not burnt, crust.)

Add the butter, if using. Turn the heat to medium. When it is melted, add the onions and garlic, stirring it constantly until it is dark golden, about 2 minutes. Add the sweet pepper and tomato, scraping the bottom of the pan with a spatula. Cook for 4 minutes until it is well blended and thickened.

Return the beef along with its juices to the pan. Mix well and add the water. Bring it to a boil over high heat, then cover and reduce the heat to low. Simmer until the meat is tender, 2½ hours. Add the potatoes, carrots and remaining 1 teaspoon of salt. Stir, cover, and cook for 30 more minutes.

VARIATION

For a spicier version, add a whole Scotch bonnet pepper along with the vegetables.

BEEF AND OKRA

MAKES 6 SERVINGS

This dish is really a stew and if you make it ahead, the taste improves. It hints of the Lebanese/Syrian influence, which along with African, Arawak Indian, Spanish, English, East Indian and Chinese form the dominant influences in Jamaican cooking. It is adjusted from a recipe by Jamaican food historian Norma Benghiat.

2 pounds shoulder steak
1 teaspoon salt
½ teaspoon freshly ground black pepper
3 tablespoons vegetable oil
2 tablespoons butter
1 medium onion, sliced
1 clove garlic, minced
2 tomatoes, chopped
1 teaspoon dried thyme
¾ cup water
1 pound okra, chopped (2 cups)

Slice the meat thinly across the grain, removing any fat and gristle. Sprinkle the salt and black pepper over the meat.

Heat the oil and butter in a large skillet over high heat. Add the beef and cook, stirring, until the moisture has evaporated and the meat is browning in the oil, 7 to 10 minutes. Add the onion and garlic and cook, stirring and scraping the bottom, for 3 minutes. Add the tomatoes and thyme and cook, stirring, for 2 minutes more. Add the water, stir and bring to a boil. Cover, reduce the heat to medium-low and simmer for 1 hour.

Add the okra and cook for 30 minutes more. Serve hot over rice.

CORNED BEEF

**MAKES 6 TO 8
SERVINGS**

*Preserved or pickled meats are a tradition in Jamaica, used out of
necessity for many years. Jamaican corned or "bully" beef is highly
spiced, which makes it a great supper served with steamed cabbage,
potatoes, horseradish and mustard in the British tradition.*

**4 pounds beef without bones, such as brisket or rump
¼ cup salt
3 teaspoons freshly ground black pepper
½ teaspoon ground nutmeg
2 teaspoons dried thyme
4 whole scallions, finely sliced
2 cloves garlic, minced
1 Scotch bonnet pepper (any color), seeded and minced
¼ teaspoon red food coloring or ½ teaspoon saltpeter
(optional)
8 cups water**

Wash the meat thoroughly with water and pat dry with paper towels. Mix
together the salt, black pepper, nutmeg and thyme in a medium bowl. In a separate bowl, blend together the scallions, garlic and Scotch bonnet pepper. Combine with the salt mixture. Mix in the food coloring or saltpeter, if using, and
mix well.

With a narrow, sharp knife, make deep slits evenly across both sides of the
meat and fill them with seasoning. Rub the remaining mixture all over the meat
until it is completely coated. Place in a clear container or a large Ziploc™ bag.
Cover or seal tightly. Leave it in the refrigerator for 3 days, turning twice daily.

When you are ready to cook, put the beef in a large pot and add enough water
to cover. Over high heat, bring it to a boil. Then reduce the heat to medium-low
and briskly simmer until tender, 1½ to 2 hours. Remove the beef from the water
to slice and serve.

POULTRY AND MEAT

POT ROAST

MAKES 6 TO 8 SERVINGS

A little pamphlet I found in the Kingston library called Cooking with Red Stripe *by Tony Gambrill places Jamaican pot roast in the same family as the classic Belgian dish carbonnade, where beer was used by Belgian peasants to tenderize less expensive cuts of beef. Here I use Jamaican Dragon Stout for an extra-rich sauce, but any beer will work perfectly well. Serve it heaped over buttered noodles.*

4 to 5 pounds top round or other economical cut of beef
2 cloves garlic, minced
½ teaspoon dry mustard
½ teaspoon dry ginger
2 teaspoons salt
1 teaspoon freshly ground black pepper
¼ cup soy sauce
¼ cup oil
1 onion, finely chopped
2 tomatoes, chopped
12 ounces beer, preferably stout
4 potatoes, chopped
2 carrots, sliced

Bring the meat to room temperature, rinse thoroughly and pat dry with a towel. Combine the garlic, mustard, ginger, salt, black pepper and soy sauce. Spread the mixture on the meat and set aside to marinate refrigerated for 1 hour.

Heat the oil in a large Dutch oven over medium heat. Add the meat and cook until browned on all sides, being careful not to burn it. Add the onion and cook until it wilts and darkens, about 5 minutes. Add the tomatoes and cook, stirring, for 2 minutes. Add the beer. Raise the heat to high and bring to a boil, then reduce the heat to low and simmer for 2 to 3 hours, adding water as needed. Add the potatoes and carrots and cook, covered, until the vegetables are tender and the meat is easily cut, about 30 minutes.

VARIATION
Use whatever other root vegetables you have on hand, if desired.

JERK PORK

MAKES 6 TO 8 SERVINGS

Boasting a high number of "special" ingredients carries some weight among the authorities, yet I have equal results with my simple, essential version. All you need is a grill with a tight-fitting lid, ice-cold Red Stripe beer and a thumping reggae beat. Everyone will be happy. Serve it with plenty of extra sauce and roast yam or bread or Festival (page 19).

5 bunches scallions, finely chopped
3 large cloves garlic, minced
3 Scotch bonnet peppers (any color), minced
2 large sprigs fresh thyme or 2 tablespoons dried
¼ cup ground allspice (dry pimento berries)
2 tablespoons freshly ground black pepper
1½ tablespoons salt
1 cup water
6 to 8 pounds pork shoulder, boned and butterflied

Combine all of the ingredients except water and pork in a large bowl. Mix well and add enough water to form a loose paste.

Put 2½ cups of the sauce in another large bowl and add the pork. (Reserve the remaining sauce for serving.) Spread the sauce all over the meat and marinate, refrigerated, for at least 1 hour or as long as 24 hours (the longer the better), turning occasionally.

Prepare an outdoor barbecue as usual, using plenty of coals. Meanwhile soak small sticks or hardwood chips in water for 30 minutes. Pimento is preferred, but any wood without a strong flavor is fine. (Mesquite conflicts with jerk's own flavor.) When the coals have become gray and well ashed over, add the soaked wood.

Place the meat on the grill and cover, leaving the vent holes slightly open. The pork should cook very slowly for about 2½ hours. Check the fire after 1 hour and add a few coals and wood as needed. Baste every 30 minutes with the marinade. Turn the meat several times as it cooks. The meat is cooked when it is firm to the touch and slightly charred.

Remove the meat from the fire and let it sit on a cutting board for 15 minutes with foil loosely placed on top. Using a cleaver, chop the meat into bite-size pieces. Serve on a large platter, doused with some of the reserved jerk sauce.

VARIATION

Any leftover meat can be shredded and mixed with jerk sauce and served on a sandwich or cracker for appetizers.

ROAST PORK

**MAKES 6 TO 8
SERVINGS**

This oven roast utilizes an economical cut of meat, making it great for a large group. Boning the meat makes slicing easier and the cooking time quicker, and the pork bone can be used to enrich your next pot of beans for another complete meal. Serve roast pork sliced with rice, Avocado Salad (page 38) and homemade Pawpaw (papaya) or Mango Chutney (pages 104 and 105).

One 7-pound pork roast (shoulder or butt)
8 scallions, chopped
3 cloves garlic, minced
1 Scotch bonnet pepper (any color), seeded and minced
1 tablespoon salt
2 teaspoons freshly ground black pepper
1 tablespoon ground allspice (dry pimento berries)
1 teaspoon cinnamon
½ teaspoon ground nutmeg
½ teaspoon ground ginger or 1 teaspoon freshly grated
1 tablespoon Pickapeppa Sauce or Worcestershire sauce
2 tablespoons water

Rinse the meat thoroughly with water and pat dry with paper towels. Using a sharp, narrow knife, remove the bone by making a long cut on one side from top to bottom down to the bone. Cut along as close to the outline of the bone as possible until the bone is free. Wrap the bone and store it in the freezer for another use. You should have about 4½ pounds of boned meat.

Combine the remaining ingredients in a bowl. Cut the meat as needed for it to lie flat (butterflied). Make slits in the meat with a knife and fill them with some of the seasoning. Rub the remaining seasoning over the rest of the meat. Place the meat in a roasting pan and cover. Marinate in the refrigerator for at least 5 hours.

Preheat the oven to 300°F. Roast the meat, uncovered, for 1 hour. Raise the heat to 450°F and roast for 20 minutes more. Remove from the oven and let rest 10 minutes before serving.

CURRIED GOAT

MAKES 6 SERVINGS

Jamaican curried goat is a national favorite. It's often served for special occasions and found at roadside stands in Mandeville, a pleasantly cool, lush hill town that is the capital of Manchester Parish located in south central Jamaica.

Curry preparations grew out of a small Indian population in the nineteenth century, brought over to Jamaica to substitute for African slaves, who had become too costly for the European plantation owners after the abolition of slavery. The Indian indentured laborers cooked and ate curried goat, a meat shunned by the English, who nevertheless were familiar with curry from their early colonization of India. Serve this spicy dish with a chutney, Fried Plantain (page 46) and white rice.

**2 pounds goat meat or beef without bones, such as
    chuck, cubed**
Juice of 1 lime
1 tablespoon salt
1 teaspoon freshly ground black pepper
1 Scotch bonnet pepper (any color), seeded and minced
½ teaspoon dried thyme
½ teaspoon ground allspice (dry pimento berries)
3 tablespoons curry powder
2 whole scallions, sliced
1 onion, sliced
3 cloves garlic, minced
¼ cup vegetable oil
3 tomatoes, diced
7 cups water
½ cup coconut milk (optional)

Rinse the goat meat and rub it all over with the juice from half of the lime. Put the meat in a large bowl and add the salt, black pepper, Scotch bonnet pepper, thyme, allspice, curry powder, scallions, onion and garlic. Leave it to marinate, refrigerated, for at least 2 hours.

Heat the oil in a large skillet over medium-high heat until it is very hot. Add the meat to the skillet, reserving the seasoning mixture, and cook until golden brown on all sides, about 6 minutes. Add the seasoning mixture to the skillet and cook, stirring, for 2 minutes. Add the tomatoes and cook until everything is well combined, about 3 more minutes. Add the water and coconut milk and bring to a boil. Reduce the heat to low, cover the skillet and cook until the meat is tender, about 2 hours. Stir in the remaining lime juice and serve with rice. This dish can be made in advance and reheated with a little extra water.

FISH AND SEAFOOD

BROWN STEW FISH

**MAKES 4 TO 6
SERVINGS**

I was served this typical breakfast at Kingslee's restaurant in Port Antonio, along with green bananas, dumplings, limeade and a cup of Blue Mountain coffee. Such fare is a common morning meal in Jamaica. Try it for supper along with Turned Cornmeal (page 16) and Callaloo (page 40).

**3 pounds fish fillets or steaks, such as king fish,
   red snapper or monkfish
Juice of 3 limes
½ cup vegetable oil
1½ onions, sliced
3 cloves garlic, minced
3 tomatoes, chopped
5 slices Scotch bonnet pepper (any color)
10 allspice berries (dry pimento berries)
   or ½ teaspoon ground
⅓ cup parsley
2 cups water
1½ teaspoons salt
½ teaspoon freshly ground black pepper**

Rinse the fish well and douse it with the fresh lime juice. Pat it dry with paper towels.

Heat the oil in a large skillet over high heat until it is very hot (you will begin to see wisps of smoke). Add the fish to the skillet in batches if necessary to avoid crowding the pan and cook until browned on both sides, about 4 minutes per side. Remove the fish and carefully pour off the excess oil.

Return the skillet to the stovetop, reduce the heat to medium and add the onions, garlic, tomatoes, Scotch bonnet pepper, allspice berries and parsley. Cook, stirring, for 1 minute. Add the water, salt and black pepper. Raise the heat to high and bring to a boil. Then reduce the heat to low, cover, and cook until sauce is thickened, 10 to 15 minutes.

FISH PIE

Another economical and easy preparation, this makes a nice luncheon dish served with Quick-Fried Cabbage (page 39).

1 pound fish fillets, such as turbot or any nonbony fish
¾ cup plain bread crumbs
1 dash hot sauce
½ teaspoon Worcestershire sauce
1 teaspoon fresh lime juice
1 clove garlic, minced
½ teaspoon salt
¼ teaspoon freshly ground black pepper
1 egg
1 cup coconut milk

Preheat the oven to 400°F. Place the fish fillets in a skillet and add enough water to cover. Cook over medium-low heat until the fish is cooked through, about 4 minutes. Remove the fish from the pan, let cool and flake it. You should have about 2 cups.

Put the flaked fish into a bowl and mix in the bread crumbs, hot sauce, Worcestershire sauce, lime juice, garlic, salt and black pepper. In another bowl, beat together the egg and coconut milk. Fold into the fish mixture. Put it into a greased 8-inch pie plate or cake pan and bake for 25 to 30 minutes or until the top is golden.

VARIATION
Capers and minced red onions can be added to the mixture for extra flavor.

FRIED FISH
AND BAMMY

MAKES 2 SERVINGS

Gloria's Rendezvous in the easy haven of Port Royal at the entrance to Kingston harbor is famous for its fried fish and bammy. Port Royal used to be known, in the buccaneer days of the seventeenth century, as the "wickedest city in the world." On the streets at night townsfolk are casually grouped together, engaged in languorous activities like dominoes and jump rope.

While waiting for our fish, we usually stroll down to The Angler's Club bar for Red Stripes and bags of tiny, dried pepper shrimp. We wander back to Gloria's through the soft ocean breeze, beers in hand, past the community gardens and curbside fish ladies selling escoveitch fish.

At home this can be almost as good with the freshest fish, hottest oil and most tolerantly nosed housemates. Serve with Vinegar Pepper Sauce (page 102) and a pitcher of iced Limeade (page 110). Bammy, the original Arawak bread made from grated sweet cassava, is rarely homemade but obtained from bammy ladies who sell these flat, circular breads in packages on the roadside—they are served steamed or fried with fish. See Ingredients and Procedures (page xxii) for the mail-order address for bammy.

**Two ¾-pound whole fish, such as snapper or any
    mild-flavored fish, gutted, heads and tails left on
Juice of 1 lime
½ teaspoon salt
¼ teaspoon freshly ground black pepper
½ cup vegetable oil
4 bammy, soaked or 4 Johnny Cakes (page 20)
4 slices sweet red pepper
6 slices onion**

Rinse the fish thoroughly inside and out with water. Rub the lime all over the fish. Pat it dry with a paper towel. Slash each fish diagonally down to the bone, twice on each side. Season with the salt and black pepper.

In a large skillet, heat the oil over medium-high heat until it is very hot (almost smoking). Carefully place both of the fish in the pan and tilt the pan slightly to distribute the oil underneath the fish and prevent them from sticking. Cook until the fish are a deep golden brown, about 4 minutes. Using 2 spatulas, gently turn the fish and cook for 5 minutes more. Put the cooked fish onto a paper towel to drain off the fat. In the same pan, fry the soaked bammy in the fish fat for 3 minutes per side. Remove from the pan and drain on paper towels. Serve the fish and bammy immediately, garnished with the sweet pepper and onion slices.

VARIATION
For escoveitch fish, pour Vinegar Pepper Sauce over the fried fish. Refrigerate for up to 12 hours.

ROAST JERK FISH

MAKES 4 SERVINGS

Fish is a modern jerk preparation—it doesn't stand up to the long smoking process required for meat. The Pork Pit Jerk Center in Montego Bay, largely responsible for introducing jerk to the tourist mainstream, devised a fish specialty to compensate for the blow Hurricane Gilbert dealt Jamaica's poultry industry. It is a whole fish stuffed with callaloo and roasted inside foil.

FOR THE JERK SAUCE

15 whole scallions
3 Scotch bonnet peppers (any color)
3 cloves garlic
1 tablespoon Pickapeppa Sauce or Worcestershire sauce
1 tablespoon soy sauce
½ teaspoon grated nutmeg
1 teaspoon dry ginger or 1 tablespoon fresh grated
    ginger
½ teaspoon ground allspice (dry pimento berries)
1 cinnamon stick, crushed
3 tablespoons white vinegar
1 teaspoon salt
3 tablespoons water

FOR THE STUFFING

2 pounds callaloo, Swiss chard or spinach
1 tablespoon vegetable oil
1 tablespoon butter
1 onion, chopped
3 whole scallions, chopped
1 sprig fresh thyme or ½ teaspoon dried
½ teaspoon salt
½ teaspoon freshly ground black pepper
¼ cup water, approximately
Four 1- to 2-pound whole fish, such as tilapia or
    red snapper, cleaned
Juice of 2 limes

For the sauce, finely chop and combine (or grind together in a food processor) the scallions, Scotch bonnet peppers and garlic. Add the Pickapeppa Sauce, soy sauce, nutmeg, ginger, allspice, cinnamon, vinegar, salt and water and blend well. Set aside.

   For the stuffing, remove the small callaloo branches with leaves from the main stem and submerge the small branches in a bowl of cold water. Let it soak for a minute and remove, discarding the water. Repeat the process 2 more times. Finely chop the leaves and branches and set aside.

Heat the oil and butter in a medium-size skillet over medium heat until the butter is melted. Add the onion and scallions and cook, stirring, until the onion begins to soften, about 2 minutes. Add the callaloo, thyme, salt and black pepper. Stir to combine, add the water and cover. Cook until the stems are tender, about 8 minutes. Remove from the heat and allow to cool.

Prepare an outdoor barbecue as usual or preheat the oven to 350°F. Rinse the fish well, pat dry with paper towels, and rub the juice from the limes on it. Pat dry with paper towels again. Make a few slices in the skin of each fish. Rub some jerk sauce on the inside and outside of the fish. Place some of the callaloo stuffing inside the cavity of each fish. Wrap them individually in foil. You can prepare the fish in advance to this stage.

Roast fish over the barbecue or in the oven for 20 to 30 minutes, depending on the size of the fish. Serve inside the foil packets with extra jerk sauce on the side.

NOTE Boneless fish fillets or steaks can be used. Place the stuffing on top of the fish and reduce the cooking time by half.

STEAMED FISH

**MAKES 4 TO 6
SERVINGS**

The tradition continues at Flo's number one fish and bammy shack in Hellshire Beach outside Kingston. Flo presides as her mother did before her. Her warm smile belies her feminine strength, which forms the backbone of Jamaican life. Working in an effortless unison, Flo and Carl (the chef) regulate the fire temperature and tend to the cooking. They freely share their methods, which are highly evolved yet simple in form.

Saturday and Sunday breakfast at Hellshire Beach is an old-time family activity for Kingstonians. Flo cooks to order. No yam? Extra pepper? No problem. Just pick your fresh fish and leave it to the masters. It's an all-in-one meal, served with yellow yam and the optional steamed bammy.

Two whole 2-pound or one 5-pound fish, such as
    red snapper
3 teaspoons salt
1 teaspoon freshly ground black pepper
12 cups water (more or less depending on the quantity
    of fish)
1½ pounds pumpkin, peeled and chopped (about 5 cups)
3 scallions, cut in 1-inch pieces
7 okra, cut in 1-inch pieces
3 slices Scotch bonnet pepper (any color)
1 large sprig fresh thyme or 2 teaspoons dried
Four ½-inch-wide slices peeled yellow yam
2 tablespoons butter
10 allspice berries (dry pimento berries) (optional)
4 bammy or dumplings (optional)

Rinse the fish and pat dry with paper towels. With a small, sharp knife, make 3 vertical slits across the flesh. Season both sides (rub inside the slit) with 1 teaspoon of the salt and black pepper. Cover and set aside at room temperature.

Place the water and pumpkin in a large pot that has a snug-fitting lid. Bring to a boil over high heat and cook until the pumpkin becomes soft, about 30 minutes, crushing it with a large spoon against the side of the pot.

In a bowl, combine the scallions, okra, Scotch bonnet pepper and thyme. Set aside.

Add the yam to the pot and boil for 15 minutes more, continuing to crush the pumpkin. Add the scallion mixture and stir. Add the butter, the remaining 2 teaspoons of salt and allspice and stir to combine.

Gently place the fish into the pot (it should be barely covered with liquid). Spoon some broth over the top of the fish. Cover and cook briskly for 10 minutes per inch of fish (measured at the thickest part of the fish). Add the bammy, placing it next to the fish, alongside the yam with 5 to 10 minutes of cooking time left.

Lift the fish onto a large platter. Place the yam and the bammy around it. Spoon the liquid over the fish. Serve steaming hot.

STEWED FISH

MAKES 6 SERVINGS

This lightly seasoned, boneless fish recipe is an excellent choice for kids and adults who don't like things too spicy! Serve with white rice, sliced tomatoes and Cole Slaw (page 44).

1½ pounds boneless fish fillet
Juice of 1 lime
¾ teaspoon salt
¼ teaspoon ground white pepper
¼ teaspoon ground allspice (dry pimento berries)
3 whole scallions, sliced
½ small onion, thinly sliced
½ cup milk
1 tablespoon all-purpose flour
1 cup water
¼ teaspoon Worcestershire sauce
¼ cup vegetable oil

Rinse the fish and pat dry with paper towels. Cut the fish into 6 equal pieces and squeeze the lime over both sides of each piece. Sprinkle the salt, white pepper and allspice evenly over all sides of the fish and place on a large plate. Distribute the scallions and onion over the top of the fish, cover and let it season for 30 minutes.

Meanwhile, in a 2-cup pitcher or bowl, gradually mix 3 tablespoons of the milk into the flour to make a smooth paste. Add the remaining milk, water, and Worcestershire sauce and blend until well combined. Set aside.

Heat the oil in a large skillet over medium-high heat until it is very hot. Place the fish, skin side up, along with the seasonings, into the hot oil. Cook on one side until golden brown, about 2 minutes. Turn each piece and cook until golden, about 1 more minute.

Slowly add the flour-milk mixture to the pan, scraping the bottom with a heat-proof spatula. Reduce the heat to medium-low, turn the fish again and simmer gently, uncovered, until the sauce thickens, about 3 minutes. Cover and cook it for another 3 to 4 minutes or until the fish is cooked through.

VEGETABLE-STUFFED FISH IN FOIL

MAKES 4 SERVINGS

Any Jamaican would use a whole fish for this 'cause the head and the cheeks in particular taste the best. The bone carries all the flavor. Since many people elsewhere prefer a boneless fillet or steak, this recipe is easily prepared by placing the stuffing on top of the fillet and cutting the cooking time in half. It makes a neat presentation by opening the foil, spooning some white rice next to the fish and placing the foil "boat" on a plate. It's a mess-free, complete meal in one.

Four 2-pound whole fish, such as red snapper
Juice of 1 lime
½ teaspoon salt
¼ teaspoon freshly ground black pepper
1 potato, diced
¼ pound pumpkin, peeled and diced (about ½ cup)
½ cup peeled and chopped yellow yam
½ cup sliced okra
½ pound lightly steamed callaloo or spinach, drained
     and chopped
2 whole scallions, chopped
1 teaspoon dried thyme
½ Scotch bonnet pepper (any color), seeded and minced
4 teaspoons butter or margarine, softened

Rinse the fish thoroughly in cold water and pat dry with paper towels. Make 2 diagonal slits on both sides of the fish. Rub the lime juice all over the fish, inside and out. Sprinkle ¼ teaspoon of the salt and the black pepper on it and set it aside.

In a steamer basket, steam the potato, pumpkin, yam and okra for 5 minutes. In a large bowl, combine the steamed vegetables with the callaloo, scallions, thyme, Scotch bonnet pepper and the remaining salt.

Grease four 1-foot square pieces of aluminum foil with butter. Put a fish on each piece of the foil and place some vegetable stuffing inside the cavity, packing it snugly. Close the foil by crimping the two sides and the ends together.

The foil-wrapped fish may be cooked on a grill, inside a 350°F oven or inside a covered pot on the stove top over medium-high heat. Regardless of the cooking method, the fish will be cooked through in 20 to 30 minutes.

NOTE For entertaining, prepare the foil envelopes in advance and cook it right before serving.

ACKEE AND
SALT FISH

**MAKES 6 TO 8
SERVINGS**

*Jamaica's national dish features the mild ackee fruit whose flesh
resembles scrambled eggs in both taste and texture. It teams up
beautifully with the salty, toothsome fish.*

*Jamaicans consume more ackee than any other Caribbean
people. In fact, "Jamaica Poisoning" is a potentially lethal condi-
tion caused from eating an immature or overripe ackee.*

*It must be picked when the pod has turned red and is com-
pletely split open, exposing the black seed and yellow flesh (the
edible part is known as the aril).*

*This dish is traditionally served at breakfast along with dump-
lings, Johnny Cakes (page 20) or other starchy foods.*

½ **pound salt cod, soaked in water to cover overnight,
refrigerated**
2 **dozen ackee**
3 **tablespoons vegetable oil**
1 **onion, sliced**
1 **tomato, chopped**
¼ **teaspoon salt, or to taste**
½ **teaspoon freshly ground black pepper**
2 **slices Scotch bonnet pepper (any color), seeded and
minced (optional)**

Drain and rinse the salt cod. Place it in a large pot of boiling fresh water and cook
for 15 minutes. When cool, flake it into small pieces and set it aside.

Clean the ackee by removing the black seed and pink membrane found in the
yellow crease of the flesh. Bring another large pot of water to a boil, add the
cleaned ackee, and cook for 5 minutes.

In a large skillet, heat the oil over medium-high heat. Add the onion and
tomato and cook, stirring, until the onion softens, about 3 minutes. Add the salt
cod, ackee, salt, black pepper and Scotch bonnet pepper, if using. To avoid break-
ing up the ackee, stir it gently until it is cooked through and the flavors are well
blended, about 5 minutes.

VARIATION
You can substitute bacon for the salt cod or omit the salt cod altogether.

CABBAGE AND
SALT COD

MAKES 6 SERVINGS

At New Mother Earth, a restaurant in Kingston, many classic Jamaican dishes are prepared with a healthful, distinctive twist— the use of whole grains and a creative touch from the hands of proprietor Mrs. Adams. This no-nonsense, wholesome stew was served with boiled green bananas, yam and a whole wheat dumpling, collectively referred to as "food."

New Mother Earth serves a variety of patties, such as ackee, chickpea and callaloo, in whole wheat pastry. They also serve fresh juices and a full array of vegetarian fare, not to mention stout cake.

½ **pound salt cod, soaked in water to cover overnight or up to 3 days refrigerated, changing the water daily**
3 **tablespoons vegetable oil**
1 **onion, chopped**
1 **whole scallion, sliced**
1 **tomato, chopped**
½ **Scotch bonnet pepper (any color), seeded and sliced**
1 **whole Scotch bonnet pepper (any color)**
1 **sprig fresh thyme or** ½ **teaspoon dried**
½ **teaspoon salt**
¼ **teaspoon freshly ground black pepper**
1 **small head cabbage, cored and shredded**
3 **tablespoons water**

Rinse and drain the salt cod. Place in a steamer basket in a large pot of simmering water and steam lightly until it is soft enough to flake, about 5 minutes.

Heat the oil in a large skillet over medium-high heat until it is very hot. Add the onion and scallion and cook, stirring, for 30 seconds. Add the tomato, sliced and whole Scotch bonnet pepper, thyme, salt, black pepper, cabbage, salt cod and water. Mix everything together completely, lower the heat to low and simmer it, covered, until the cabbage is tender, for 20 to 30 minutes. Remove the whole Scotch bonnet pepper before serving.

CALLALOO AND SALT COD

MAKES 6 TO 8 SERVINGS

Serve this complete meal with Boiled Green Bananas (page 44), rice or dumplings.

½ pound salt cod, soaked in water to cover overnight, refrigerated
2 pounds callaloo or any other sturdy green such as Swiss chard, mustard or dandelion greens
6 tablespoons vegetable oil
2 onions, chopped
2 tomatoes, chopped
¼ cup water
1 whole Scotch bonnet pepper (any color)

Drain and rinse the salt cod. Place in a large pot of boiling water and cook for 15 minutes. Remove the salt cod from the water, cool and flake it into small pieces. Set aside.

Meanwhile, clean the callaloo. Remove the small branches with leaves and discard the main stem. Submerge the callaloo in a bowl of cold water. Let it soak for a minute and remove, discarding the water. Repeat 2 more times. Finely chop the leaves and stalks and set aside.

Heat the oil in a large skillet over medium-high heat. Add the onions and tomatoes to the skillet and cook, stirring, for 2 minutes. Add the fish, callaloo, water and Scotch bonnet pepper. Cook until the greens are tender, about 15 minutes, remove Scotch bonnet pepper and serve immediately.

SALT COD STEW

**MAKES 6 TO 8
SERVINGS**

Used in so many preparations in Jamaica, salt cod has a wonderful texture and is perfectly suited for stew. Serve in a large bowl with a scoop of rice and Avocado Salad (page 38).

1 pound salt cod, soaked in water to cover overnight,
    refrigerated
Juice of 1 lime
¼ cup vegetable oil
2 onions, chopped
4 whole scallions, sliced
3 tomatoes, diced
1 sprig fresh thyme or 1 teaspoon dried thyme
½ teaspoon freshly ground black pepper
4 slices Scotch bonnet pepper (any color)
½ cup water
2 carrots, sliced
2 potatoes, peeled and sliced
½ cup sliced okra

Drain and rinse the salt cod. Pat dry with paper towels and cut into small pieces. Place in a bowl and pour the lime juice over it. Set aside.

Heat the oil in a large skillet over medium-high heat until it is very hot. Add the onions and scallions and cook, stirring, for 2 minutes. Add the tomatoes and continue cooking for another 2 minutes. Add the thyme, black pepper, Scotch bonnet pepper and water. Bring to a boil and add the carrots, potatoes, okra and fish. Cover the pan and reduce the heat to medium-low. Cook at a brisk simmer until the fish is cooked and the vegetables are tender, 15 to 20 minutes.

MACKEREL RUN DOWN

In this traditional dish, the liquid boils out of the coconut milk and "runs down" into a thick consistency. Salt cod may be used instead of mackerel. Serve with Boiled Green Bananas (page 44).

1½ pounds pickled mackerel fillet or any pickled
    fish, soaked in water to cover for 3 to 6 hours,
    refrigerated
Juice of 1 lime
1 coconut, freshly grated (2 to 3 cups) or 3 cups coconut
    milk
3 cups boiling water
1 onion, chopped
2 cloves garlic, minced
1 small Scotch bonnet pepper (any color), seeded
    and minced
2 tomatoes, chopped
1 teaspoon salt
½ teaspoon freshly ground black pepper
1 teaspoon dried thyme
1 tablespoon white vinegar

Drain, rinse and flake the mackerel. Put the fish in a bowl and pour the lime juice over it. Set aside. Put the coconut in a large bowl and pour the boiling water over it. Let sit for 10 minutes. Drain out the coconut milk and put it in a medium-size saucepan. Bring to a boil over high heat. Let cook until it is oily and slightly thickened, about 8 minutes.

Reduce the heat to medium, add the onion and garlic to the coconut milk and cook until tender, about 3 minutes. Add the Scotch bonnet pepper, tomatoes, salt and black pepper and continue cooking for 8 minutes. Add the fish to the saucepan, and cook for an additional 10 minutes. Add the thyme and vinegar. Serve immediately.

COCONUT SHRIMP

**MAKES 6 TO 8
SERVINGS**

*The nutty toasted coconut complements the shrimp flavor perfectly.
This makes a great appetizer served with the spicy dipping sauce.*

FOR THE SAUCE
2 teaspoons Scotch bonnet pepper (any color), seeded
    and minced
Juice of 1 lime
1 tablespoon honey
1 tablespoon dark rum
½ teaspoon salt
1 tablespoon vegetable oil

FOR THE SHRIMP
1 pound medium shrimp, peeled and deveined
2 egg whites
½ teaspoon Worcestershire sauce
¼ teaspoon salt
1 cup shredded, unsweetened coconut
½ cup vegetable oil

For the sauce, combine the Scotch bonnet pepper, lime juice, honey, rum, salt and oil in a serving bowl. Set aside.

Rinse the shrimp in cold water and pat dry with paper towels. In a small bowl, beat together the egg whites, Worcestershire sauce and salt. Spread the coconut out on a plate. Coat each shrimp with the egg white mixture and roll in the coconut.

Heat ¼ cup of the oil in a large skillet over high heat until it is very hot. Add half of the shrimp to the oil in a single layer. Fry until golden brown, for 1½ minutes. Turn each one over and cook an additional 2 minutes. Remove to drain on paper towels. Using the remaining ¼ cup of oil, repeat the process until all of the shrimp is cooked. Serve the shrimp immediately with the dipping sauce.

CURRY SHRIMP

MAKES 6 SERVINGS   *This recipe is from Erryll, a.k.a. Float, a.k.a. Cock Upon the Water, a fisherman down in Bluefields on the south coast. The recipe is simply stated as follows: "Burn de curry in h'oil, add de seasoning, okra, shrimp and water. H'allow to cook far a shart while." Eaten on a riverbank, after catching the shrimp and cooking it over an open fire, this is a true experience! Serve with rice, Mango Chutney (page 105) and Mixed Greens (page 43).*

3 tablespoons oil
2 tablespoons curry powder
1 medium-size onion, chopped
1 whole scallion, chopped
1 clove garlic, minced
3 tablespoons sweet red pepper, seeded and diced
1 slice Scotch bonnet pepper (any color)
¼ teaspoon freshly ground black pepper
3 tablespoons tomato sauce or paste
1 cup water
1 cup sliced okra
1 pound medium-size shrimp, peeled and deveined

Heat the oil in a large skillet over medium-high heat. When it is very hot, add the curry powder. Cook, stirring, for 2 minutes. Add the onion, scallion, garlic, sweet pepper, Scotch bonnet pepper and black pepper. Cook, stirring constantly, for 3 minutes. Add the tomato sauce or paste and cook 3 minutes more. Add the water and blend well.

Add the okra and shrimp. Reduce the heat to medium, cover and cook until the shrimp are just cooked through, about 5 minutes. It is best served hot, straight out of the pan.

NOTE   The shrimp heads, tails and shells can be left on for better flavor and a more rustic dining experience.

PEPPER SHRIMP

If you happen to be traveling in Jamaica in the Parish of St. Elizabeth near the town of Black River, be prepared to stop by the side of the road in Middle Quarters, where the shrimp ladies sell small bags of river shrimp cooked with Scotch bonnet pepper. Try this as blazingly hot as you can stand it with a cold drink not too far from your reach. This makes a great appetizer for a feisty crowd.

**1 pound small shrimp, unpeeled with heads and tails
      left on
3 tablespoons salt
¼ cup water
4 Scotch bonnet peppers (any color), seeded and minced**

Place the shrimp and salt into a medium-size saucepan and mix gently with your hands. Add the water. Distribute the minced Scotch bonnet peppers evenly over the shrimp. Over high heat, bring the shrimp to a boil, then cover the pan and cook for 4 minutes, stirring after each minute, or until the shrimp are pink and cooked through. Remove from the heat and chill before serving.

NOTE You can make this much less spicy by adding 1 whole Scotch bonnet pepper instead of 4 minced.

LOBSTER CURRY

Best cooked at the seaside when there's an abundance of lobsters, this dish is especially suited for the spiny lobster, which has no claws but a tail chock-full of delicious meat. American lobster is a fine substitute. Serve with fluffy white rice and a cold vegetable salad.

2 fresh lobsters
3 tablespoons vegetable oil
2 whole scallions, finely sliced
2 cloves garlic, crushed
2 slices Scotch bonnet pepper (any color)
½ teaspoon dried thyme
½ teaspoon salt
¼ teaspoon freshly ground black pepper
4 teaspoons curry powder

In a large pot with 3 to 4 quarts of boiling water, boil the lobsters for 5 minutes per pound. Remove the lobster meat from the shells, cut into bite-size pieces and set aside.

In a large skillet, heat the oil over medium-high heat. When it is hot, add the scallions, garlic, Scotch bonnet pepper, thyme, salt and black pepper. Cook, stirring, for 1 minute, being careful not to burn it. Increase the heat to high, add the curry powder and cook, stirring, for 1 minute until it changes color. Place the lobster meat in the pan and stir to blend with the seasonings for 30 seconds. Remove the pan from the heat. Remove the Scotch bonnet slices and discard them. Serve immediately.

NOTE This dish can be chilled and served as a salad over fresh lettuce leaves.

CURRY CRAB AND DUMPLINGS

**MAKES 6 TO 8
SERVINGS**

This recipe comes from a Trinidadian cook named Michelle Jackson, who gets rave reviews from her Jamaican friends every time she prepares it.

Juice of 2 limes
15 crabs, cleaned (see Note)
1 onion, chopped
1 whole scallion, sliced
2 tomatoes, chopped
1 sweet green or red pepper, chopped
1 Scotch bonnet pepper (any color)
4 cloves garlic, peeled
4 tablespoons curry powder
4 sprigs fresh thyme or 2 teaspoons dried
1½ tablespoons freshly ground black pepper
2 teaspoons salt
3 tablespoons vegetable oil
2 cups coconut milk
1 to 2 cups water

FOR THE FLOUR DUMPLINGS
2 cups all-purpose flour
½ teaspoon salt
⅔ cup water

Place the lime juice and the rinds in a very large bowl. Add the crabs and enough water to cover them. Soak the crabs in the lime water for 15 minutes. Drain and rinse them.

Season the crabs for 1 hour by placing them in a very large bowl along with the onion, scallion, tomatoes, sweet pepper, Scotch bonnet pepper, whole garlic, 2 tablespoons of the curry powder, thyme, black pepper and salt.

Heat the oil in a large pot over medium heat. Add the remaining 2 tablespoons of curry powder and cook, stirring, for 5 seconds. Add the crabs along with their seasonings. Cook, stirring, for 2 minutes. Add the coconut milk and enough water to fully cover the crabs. Raise the heat to high and boil briskly, loosely covered, for 1 hour or until the sauce thickens.

Meanwhile, prepare the dumplings. In a medium-size bowl, combine the flour and salt. Stir in the water to distribute it evenly into the flour. With your hands, knead it to form a soft and smooth dough. Roll out the dough into a fat snake shape and cut it into 12 pieces. Form each dumpling into a ball and indent it slightly in the center. Boil them in a pot of salted water for 15 minutes.

To serve, place a couple of cooked dumplings in each bowl and spoon some crabs and sauce over it. The crabs will keep in the refrigerator for several days.

NOTE Cleaned crabs can be found in the frozen section of many groceries. If you are using fresh crabs, first, place them in a large heatproof container. Pour boiling water over the live crabs, covering them completely. Let sit for 5 minutes. Drain and put the crabs into the sink.

Clean each crab under running water as follows: Pinch off the ends of each leg (nails), leaving the gundy (large claw). Hold the crab in your palm with the crab's back facing down and lift off the triangle between the legs; pull it up and bring off the whole back shell that separates it from the body. Discard the shell. Take a small teaspoon and scrape the center clean of the innards. Pull off the gills on the sides. Drain and rinse the crabs in cold water. They are ready to use. The crabs may be frozen at this stage.

PICKLED SHRIMP COCKTAIL

MAKES 6 TO 8 SERVINGS AS AN APPETIZER

River shrimp or crawfish with heads and tails are perfect for this dish. Otherwise use shelled shrimp served with toothpicks and hot sauce.

1½ cups cane or apple cider vinegar
1 whole Scotch bonnet pepper (any color)
1 clove garlic, minced
1 onion, sliced
½ chocho (chayote), peeled, pitted and chopped,
    or ½ cucumber, peeled, seeded and chopped
½ teaspoon ground allspice (dry pimento berries)
3 tablespoons fresh minced ginger
¼ teaspoon salt
¼ teaspoon freshly ground black pepper
2 pounds shrimp, unpeeled with heads and tails left on

Place all of the ingredients except the shrimp into a large noncorrosive saucepan. Bring to a boil over high heat and add the shrimp. Cook for 2 minutes. Pour into a large bowl and refrigerate. Marinate for up to 12 hours before serving.

SAUCES

JERK SAUCE

The basis for righteous jerk barbecue is great sauce. Sauce varies among the experts, recipes are coveted and shrouded in secrecy, yet basic flavors dominate. Chief among them, the pimento tree has given jerking its young green branches for *patas* (grill stands) and its berries (allspice) for seasoning. In this recipe, jerk sauce is pared down to its bare essentials. Many Jamaicans have different recipes, which include cinnamon or ginger or nutmeg or you name it. Build your own sauce to taste; this is not a science, it's an art! How much fiery Scotch bonnet pepper to use is a controversy that rages among family and friends. Tested on both wimps and fire-eaters, this sauce challenges the former and leaves macho mouths clamoring, "Make it spicier next time." For them just splash in some hot pepper and line up the cold Red Stripes.

MAKES 1
QUART

5 bunches whole scallions, finely chopped
3 large cloves garlic, minced
3 Scotch bonnet peppers (any color), seeded and minced
2 large sprigs fresh thyme or 2 tablespoons dried
¼ cup ground allspice (dry pimento berries)
2 tablespoons freshly ground black pepper
1½ tablespoons salt
1 cup water

In a large bowl, combine all ingredients except the water. Mix well and add water to form a loose paste.

NOTE Sources for specialty wood chips often carry dried pimento leaves, which add additional flavor to the fire at barbecue time.

JERK SAUCE
PORTLAND STYLE

MAKES 1½ CUPS

Audley, a Jamaican chef from Port Maria who made this sauce, says that anyone who tastes his sauce says its better than that at Boston Beach in Port Antonio, the Jamaican jerk mecca. This version of jerk sauce is especially good with fish.

15 whole scallions, finely chopped
3 Scotch bonnet peppers (any color), seeded and
    finely chopped
3 cloves garlic, finely chopped
1 tablespoon Pickapeppa Sauce
1 tablespoon soy sauce
½ teaspoon grated nutmeg
1 teaspoon dry ginger or 1 tablespoon fresh grated
½ teaspoon ground allspice (dry pimento berries)
1 cinnamon stick, crushed
3 tablespoons white vinegar
1 teaspoon salt
3 tablespoons water

Combine all ingredients in a food processor. It will keep in the refrigerator for at least 1 month.

PAWPAW PEPPER SAUCE

MAKES 2½ CUPS

Many people keep their own homemade hot sauce on hand or at least a favorite commercial sauce. Jamaicans use it like ketchup. This sauce is spicy, yet flavorful, and simple to prepare. The pawpaw sweetens and texturizes the vegetable base and provides a gentle palette for the robust Scotch bonnet peppers.

3 carrots, peeled
1 chocho (chayote), peeled and pitted, or 1 medium
    cucumber, peeled and seeded
6 Scotch bonnet peppers (any color)
1 small or ½ large pawpaw (papaya), peeled and seeded
2 teaspoons salt
1 teaspoon brown sugar
⅓ cup white vinegar
¾ cup water

Place the carrots and chocho in a food processor or blender. Blend until pulverized. Remove the stems from the Scotch bonnet peppers and add the peppers to the carrots and chocho. Blend until the mixture is an even consistency. Add the pawpaw, continuing to blend until you have a uniform texture.

Place the mixture into a noncorrosive saucepan. Add the salt, brown sugar, vinegar and water. Bring it to a boil over high heat, then reduce the heat to low and cover. Simmer it for 30 minutes. Remove from the heat and let cool completely. Place in small bottles or jars. Keep it refrigerated.

VINEGAR PEPPER SAUCE

MAKES 1 QUART

This is served at the table in a white bucket at Flo's, the number one fish restaurant in Hellshire Beach. It is spooned over fried fish to transform it into escoveitch fish. As an all-around table sauce, it's great spooned into soups or over broiled meats. Its taste is crisp and biting. Keep out of the reach of children!

1 large carrot
1 large white onion
3 or 4 Scotch bonnet peppers (orange recommended)
2 cups white vinegar

Slice the carrot lengthwise into strips. Stack the strips and julienne from top to bottom. Cut the onion in half, placing the cut sides down on a cutting board. Cut each piece in half lengthwise (keeping the halves together). Thinly slice each half. Carefully slice each Scotch bonnet pepper into thin slices.

Pour the vinegar into a large bowl, add all of the ingredients, and mix well.

Spoon mixture into jars and close the lid. It will keep indefinitely (if it lasts long enough!).

TOMATO RELISH

MAKES 1 QUART

It's no doubt this relish has English roots. It features Jamaica's wonderful sweet spices. It can be served as a topping for grilled snapper, it forms the basis for an excellent barbecue sauce, and it takes an everyday hot dog to a new level.

2 onions, chopped
1 sweet green pepper, seeded and chopped
9 tomatoes, chopped
½ cup sugar
1 cup white vinegar
1 tablespoon salt
1 teaspoon ground allspice (dry pimento berries)
1 teaspoon cinnamon
½ teaspoon whole cloves

Combine the onions, sweet pepper, tomatoes and sugar in a large saucepan. Place over high heat and bring to a boil. Cook until thickened, about 20 minutes. Add the vinegar, salt, allspice, cinnamon and cloves and continue to boil for 15 minutes more. Remove from the heat and let cool. Store in glass jars in the refrigerator up to 6 months.

COCKTAIL SAUCE

MAKES 1½ CUPS

Serve this sauce with any of the savory fritters.

1 cup Tomato Relish (page 103) or ketchup
½ cup mayonnaise
Juice of ½ lime
¼ to ½ teaspoon hot pepper sauce

Blend all of the ingredients together and place in a serving bowl.

PAWPAW CHUTNEY

MAKES 3 CUPS

Lime rind adds a contrasting green color to the orange pawpaw and a biting flavor complement for this subtle-tasting fruit. This chutney is perfect for any plain roasted meat or fish and is delicious alone, spooned onto a cracker or cornmeal fritter as an appetizer.

1 chocho (chayote), peeled, pitted and diced, or
    1 cucumber, peeled, seeded and diced
½ sweet red or green pepper, seeded and sliced
¼ lime, diced
2 teaspoons ginger powder
1 cup white vinegar
1½ cups sugar
3 teaspoons salt
¾ cup water
3 medium pawpaw (papaya), peeled, seeded and
    chopped (about 2 cups)

Place all the ingredients in a saucepan and cook gently over low heat for 2 hours, stirring periodically.

Remove from the heat and allow the chutney to cool. Store in glass jars in the refrigerator up to 6 months.

MANGO CHUTNEY

MAKES 3 CUPS

This chutney is a natural accompaniment for any of the curry dishes.

4 mangoes, peeled, pitted and chopped (4 cups)
3 tablespoons fresh grated ginger
1 onion, chopped
1 clove garlic, minced
½ sweet red pepper, seeded and chopped (about 1 cup)
½ cup raisins
⅓ cup sugar
2 teaspoons salt
½ cup white vinegar
⅓ cup water

Mix all of the ingredients together in a noncorrosive saucepan. Bring to a boil over high heat, then reduce the heat to low and simmer for 1 hour and 15 minutes. Remove from the heat and allow the chutney to cool. Store in glass jars in the refrigerator up to 6 months.

BARBECUE SAUCE

MAKES 3 CUPS

Old-fashioned barbecue sauce is a great item to have on hand for a quick preparation—just brush some sauce onto any meat in the final stages of grilling.

1 cup white vinegar
1 cup water
½ cup Tomato Relish (page 103) or ketchup
½ cup ketchup
6 tablespoons brown sugar
3 tablespoons Worcestershire sauce
1 tablespoon dry mustard
1½ teaspoons salt
2 cloves garlic, minced
½ teaspoon freshly ground black pepper

Combine all ingredients in a medium-size saucepan and simmer gently over low heat for 15 minutes. Store refrigerated up to 6 months.

PINEAPPLE ALMOND CHUTNEY

MAKES 1 QUART

Pineapple is a perfect fruit for chutney, with its toothsome texture and yummy sweet flavor, beautifully complemented by the crunchy almonds.

1 pineapple
1 cup white vinegar
2 cups light brown sugar
1 cup raisins
1 teaspoon salt
3 tablespoons fresh grated ginger
1 onion, chopped
1 teaspoon fresh lime juice
½ cup almonds, chopped

Wash and peel the pineapple, reserving the peels for Pineappleade (page 111). Cut the pineapple in quarters lengthwise and slice off the core on each piece. Chop the fruit into small pieces and put in a noncorrosive medium-size saucepan.

Add the vinegar, brown sugar, raisins, salt, ginger and onion. Bring to a boil over high heat, then reduce the heat to low and simmer until the mixture thickens, about 50 minutes. Stir in the lime juice and almonds. Allow it to cool completely, place in glass jars and refrigerate up to 6 months.

HARD SAUCE

MAKES 1 CUP

This sauce can accompany different puddings and fruitcakes like bread, sweet potato, or green banana, which are traditionally served at Christmas and New Year's.

¼ cup butter (½ stick)
¾ cup sugar
1 teaspoon hot water
3 tablespoons brandy, whiskey or rum

In a bowl, cream together the butter and sugar. Add the hot water and mix. Mix in the liquor and serve hot over dessert. Refrigerate up to 6 months. Reheat in a double boiler before using.

PINEAPPLE JAM

MAKES 2 CUPS

It's hard to imagine a more luscious combination than pineapple jam spread over a slice of toasted Coconut Bread (page 136). This jam also makes a good foundation for sweet-and-sour sauce or a glaze for roasted meats.

1 pineapple
1 cup water
2 cups sugar
Juice of 2 limes

Peel and grate the pineapple, reserving the peel for Pineappleade (page 111).

Grate the flesh—you should end up with about 2 cups. Put the pineapple and water in a small saucepan and cook over medium-low heat until it is soft, about 35 minutes.

Add the sugar and lime juice and stir to combine. Cook until the mixture has thickened, 45 to 60 minutes. Spoon the jam into a 16-ounce jar and seal. Keep it in the refrigerator up to 6 months.

RUM SAUCE

MAKES 2 CUPS

This is a great sauce to serve over Coconut Ice Cream (page 147).

¾ cup brown sugar
⅓ cup water
½ cup butter (1 stick)
¼ cup dark rum

Combine the sugar, water, butter and rum in a small saucepan and bring to a boil over medium-high heat. Boil gently until thickened, about 10 minutes. Cool slightly and pour a little sauce over each portion of dessert before serving. It can be refrigerated and reheated in a double boiler.

DRINKS

LIMEADE

**MAKES SIX 8-OUNCE
SERVINGS**

With the abundance of limes in Jamaica, limeade is a common drink. Even the commonly bottled unsweetened lime juice is excellent paired with bottled sugar syrup for a quick limeade. As an alternative to sugar, try honey, which combined with lime juice is an excellent aid for the respiratory system.

**5 to 7 medium-size limes
5 cups water (40 ounces)
½ cup honey or sugar**

For the maximum juice, roll the limes over the counter back and forth with the palm of your hand. Cut the limes in half and juice them by hand or with a juicer (reserving the rinds). You should have about ½ cup (4 ounces) of juice. Place the rinds and the juice in a large pitcher.

Place 1 cup of the water in a saucepan over high heat. When it boils, add the honey or sugar and mix until it dissolves. Pour this mixture into the pitcher along with the remaining water. Blend well and taste for sweetness. Refrigerate it for 1 hour. Remove the rinds and discard.

VARIATION

For super flavor and enriched medicinal value, add slices of fresh ginger into the pitcher along with the rinds.

COCONUT PINEAPPLE DRINK

**MAKES FOUR
8-OUNCE SERVINGS**

Coconut and pineapple form an unbeatable union. Coconut is an alleged kidney tonic, making this a healthy drink as well. Serve it chilled.

**4 cups water (32 ounces)
2 tablespoons sugar
3 cups fresh grated coconut
½ cup pineapple juice (4 ounces)**

Bring the water to a boil in a saucepan over high heat and pour it into a heat-proof pitcher. Add the sugar and stir until it dissolves. Add the coconut and mix. Let sit for 1 hour. Strain out the coconut shavings and add the pineapple juice. Stir well and serve chilled or over ice.

PINEAPPLEADE

**MAKES FOUR
8-OUNCE SERVINGS**

This frugal drink utilizes the peel of the pineapple. It's a sin not to make this drink every time you use the flesh of a fresh pineapple. You'll never carelessly discard the peel again once you've tasted this thirst-quenching treat.

**4 cups water (32 ounces)
1 pineapple
½ cup sugar
2 whole cloves
½-inch piece fresh grated ginger (1 teaspoon)**

Bring the water to a boil in a saucepan over high heat. Wash and peel the pineapple and place the peel, sugar, cloves and ginger into a large heatproof pitcher. (Save the rest of the pineapple for another use.) Pour the boiling water into the pitcher and stir. Let it sit at room temperature for 24 hours. Strain and serve chilled or over ice.

LIME SQUASH

**MAKES TWO
8-OUNCE DRINKS**

This refreshing carbonated drink is a great, healthy alternative to soda.

**4 small or 2 medium-size limes
3 tablespoons honey
1¼ cups carbonated water (mineral water,
    club soda, etc.) (10 ounces)**

For the maximum juice, roll the limes over the counter back and forth with the palm of your hand. Cut the limes in half and juice them by hand or with a juicer. You should have ½ cup (4 ounces) of juice. Put the juice and honey into a bowl and mix well with a wire whisk or fork. Pour the mixture into a pitcher. Add the carbonated water and stir until all of the ingredients are well combined. Taste and adjust it for the desired sweetness. Serve it over ice.

VARIATION
Lemons can be used in the place of limes.

GRAPEFRUIT-ORANGE-LIME DRINK

**MAKES TWO
8-OUNCE SERVINGS**

Grapefruits are said to have originated in the Caribbean as a natural hybrid of an orange and a shaddock, a thick-skinned, rather bitter citrus fruit brought aboard a British merchant ship from Polynesia in the mid-eighteenth century. Both grapefruits and oranges grow bountifully in Jamaica. Their flavors combined taste even better than they do alone. And the drink is packed with vitamin C.

2 grapefruits
2 oranges
1 lime
3 tablespoons honey

Cut the grapefruits, oranges and lime in half, and juice them by hand or with a juicer. Pour all of the juice into a blender jar. Add the honey and blend on high speed for 30 seconds. Pour into a pitcher and chill for at least 1 hour before serving.

VARIATION
Add grated ginger or cinnamon sticks for a spicy version.

PAWPAW DRINK

**MAKES TWO
10-OUNCE SERVINGS**

Pawpaw is the fruit that many folks know as papaya. It is an excellent digestive aid. Serve this along with any fiercely spiced meat dish.

1 ripe pawpaw (papaya)
2 oranges
1 lime
1 slice fresh ginger
3 tablespoons honey
4 ice cubes

Slice the pawpaw in half. Scoop out the seeds and discard. Scoop the flesh into a blender jar. Cut the oranges and lime in half and juice by hand or with a juicer. Add the juice to the blender jar. Add the ginger, honey and ice cubes and blend until it is well combined with a smooth, slushy texture.

MANGO SMOOTHIE

**MAKES FOUR
6-OUNCE SERVINGS**

This contemporary version of mango punch turns a wonderful fruit into an extra healthy shake with the addition of yogurt. If the mango is ripe enough without being too fibrous, the resulting texture that delivers the lime-tinged flavor is ambrosial.

1 medium-size mango
⅓ cup plain yogurt (preferably nonfat)
1½ tablespoons honey
Two 1-inch strips of lime rind
Juice of 2 oranges
3 ice cubes
4 lime wedges

Peel the mango and cut the flesh around the pit into pieces. Put the pieces in a blender jar along with the yogurt, honey, lime rind, orange juice and ice cubes. Blend on high speed until smooth. Serve with a wedge of lime as a garnish on the side of each glass.

BANANA MILK SHAKE

**MAKES FOUR
8-OUNCE SERVINGS**

Kids and adults with a penchant for bananas will love this shake. You can replace the ice cream with frozen yogurt or any of the other ice cream alternatives, but there is nothing like old-fashioned vanilla ice cream for a devilishly addictive treat. Check out the Pelican Grill in Montego Bay for the ultimate banana milk shake.

2 bananas
⅓ cup sugar
2 cups milk (16 ounces)
1 teaspoon vanilla
1 pint vanilla ice cream

Place the peeled bananas and the remaining ingredients into a blender jar. Blend on high speed until the ingredients are well combined.

PEANUT PUNCH

**MAKES FOUR
8-OUNCE SERVINGS**

Try this super protein blast for a creamy and refreshing drink.

**2 cups roasted and shelled peanuts
3 cups water (24 ounces)
1 cup milk (8 ounces)
1 teaspoon vanilla
3 tablespoons honey
¼ teaspoon grated nutmeg**

Place the peanuts and water into a blender jar and blend until the peanuts are pulverized. Strain the liquid from the ground peanuts and put the liquid back into the blender jar along with the remaining ingredients. (Discard the ground peanuts.) Beat it until it is frothy. Serve it immediately or refrigerate (blend again before serving).

GINGER BEER

**MAKES FOUR
8-OUNCE SERVINGS**

Jamaicans love their ginger beer. Without a doubt, the natural abundance of ginger on the island and its superior quality accounts for its popularity. These days ginger beer is widely available and rarely made at home. But homemade ginger beer is easy to make and just requires yeast for fermentation. It is well worth the effort.

**¼ cup fresh grated ginger
¾ cup sugar
4 cups water (32 ounces)
Juice of ½ lime
½ packet dry yeast**

Combine all of the ingredients in a large pitcher. Stir and allow to sit at room temperature for 24 hours. Strain and refrigerate. Serve chilled.

SORREL DRINK

**MAKES TWELVE
8-OUNCE SERVINGS**

No discussion of Jamaican beverages would be complete without mention of sorrel, which is a festive offering at Christmas and New Year's. This radiant red-flowering plant, a member of the hibiscus family, makes a fragrant drink with a zesty taste. It is also served with white rum as an unusual cocktail. Dried sorrel can be found packaged at specialty stores abroad. Use 3 to 4 cups if using dried leaves.

**6 cups sorrel sepals, removed from the stalk
1-inch piece fresh ginger, sliced
Three 2-inch pieces orange peel
5 allspice berries (dry pimento berries), crushed
3 whole cloves, crushed
12 cups boiling water (96 ounces)
1½ cups sugar
Juice of 1 lime**

Place the sorrel, ginger, orange peel, allspice and cloves in a large heatproof pitcher or bowl. Pour in 10 cups of the boiling water and stir. Cover and leave it to steep for 24 hours. Strain out the liquid through a sieve. Boil the remaining 2 cups of water and blend it with the sugar until dissolved. Add the sugar water to the strained liquid along with the lime juice. Stir to blend it completely. Sweeten it further if desired. Serve over crushed ice.

FRESH MINT TEA

**MAKES FOUR
8-OUNCE SERVINGS**

Growing wild in many corners of the island, mint makes a delicious and medicinal tea. It's an excellent beverage to serve with a meal because it aids in the assimilation of nutrient substances by the blood. It calms the tummy and tastes great, too.

**12 sprigs fresh mint
4 cups boiling water (32 ounces)
4 teaspoons honey**

Wash the mint and place in a large heatproof pitcher. Pour the boiling water over the mint. Allow to steep for 4 minutes. Strain and serve the tea in cups with a teaspoon of honey in each cup.

BLUE MOUNTAIN COFFEE

Coffee beans have been harvested in Jamaica for over two centuries, and today Jamaica enjoys an outstanding reputation for the quality of its coffee. It is grown on misty mountain peaks, which reach up to 7,000 feet above sea level. The right combination of soil and rain has produced an industry that ranges from the large Mavis Bank estate to small farmers and roasters whose families have been involved for generations. The acidity and sweetness of Jamaican coffee are balanced to perfection. With such cachet comes a high price tag, which makes it a wonderful gift for any serious coffee lover. Savored preciously, I prefer to make each cup to order or for a group in a drip carafe, but definitely not a percolator.

> **2 tablespoons Blue Mountain coffee, freshly ground**
> **1 cup boiling water (8 ounces)**
> **2 tablespoons milk**
> **1 teaspoon sugar**

Place the ground coffee into a paper filter that fits into a 1-cup filter funnel. Pour the boiled water through the coffee into a large mug.

In a small saucepan, heat the milk and sugar together and pour into the coffee. Serve immediately.

VARIATION
For a dessert coffee, add 2 ounces of Tia Maria (coffee liqueur) or Rumona (rum liqueur) and top with whipped cream.

FRESH GINGER TEA

**MAKES ONE
8-OUNCE SERVING**

Jamaica is so famous for its commercial production of ginger that it's sometimes referred to as the Land of Ginger. Its flavor features prominently throughout Jamaican cooking and it's also used medicinally as a cure-all. Its many proven healing properties help everything from motion sickness to fevers, colds and headaches. As a digestive aid, it's the perfect drink to serve with meals. This tea is not only good hot but is a refreshingly tangy thirst quencher served cold.

**1 tablespoon fresh grated ginger
1 cup boiling water (8 ounces)
2 teaspoons honey**

Put the grated ginger in a teapot and pour in the boiling water. Allow to steep for 4 minutes. Strain and serve the tea in cups with a teaspoon of honey in each cup.

NOTE The grated ginger can be tied in a piece of muslin or cheesecloth before placing it in the teapot so no straining is necessary. Be sure to remove the bundle before serving.

117

VARIATION

For iced tea, put the honey in a pitcher and pour the hot tea over it. Stir and refrigerate.

EGG NOG

**MAKES FOUR
5-OUNCE SERVINGS**

Served on the festive occasions of Christmas and Easter, this drink made with brandy was at one time prescribed medicinally in England in the case of "extreme weakness."

3 eggs
1 cup sugar
1 cup milk (8 ounces)
1 teaspoon vanilla
½ cup heavy cream (4 ounces)
1 cup dark rum (8 ounces)
¼ teaspoon ground nutmeg

Separate the yolks and the whites of the eggs. In a large bowl, beat the egg whites and sugar together to form soft peaks and set aside. In another bowl, beat the yolks until they are frothy. Add the milk and vanilla and mix. In another bowl, beat the cream until it is thickened.

Add the cream to the egg whites and gently fold them together. Fold in the egg yolk–milk mixture and the rum, blending until the mixture is well combined. Serve the egg nog in glasses over ice with nutmeg on top.

RUM PUNCH

**MAKES FIVE
8-OUNCE SERVINGS**

Several years ago, we arrived at this simple formula after tasting and testing many versions for a Jamaican restaurant. It's a rough job, but someone has to do it. Try creating your own by mixing a few different fruit juices with your favorite rum.

2¼ cups unsweetened pineapple juice (18 ounces)
2 cups guava juice (16 ounces)
Juice of 3 medium-size limes
½ cup dark Jamaican rum (4 ounces)

Mix all of the ingredients well and chill. Serve over ice, dressed with tropical fruit. Splash on an extra hit of rum before serving if desired.

BANANA DAIQUIRI

**MAKES TWO
8-OUNCE SERVINGS**

*This frozen drink is a happy hour favorite at north coast resorts.
It tastes like dessert and slides down so smoothly, but beware of the
creeping rum sensation.*

¾ cup rum (6 ounces)
1½ ripe bananas, peeled
Juice of 1 lime
1 strip lime rind
3½ tablespoons sugar
10 ice cubes

Combine all of the ingredients in a blender jar and blend on high speed until the
texture is smooth. Serve in glasses with a lime wedge and an extra splash of rum.

MANGO LIQUEUR

**MAKES 3 TO 4
QUARTS**

*Summer in Jamaica brings the mango season. This homemade
brew is perfect for any lucky soul who happens to have extra fresh
mangoes hanging around that haven't been gobbled up. It makes
a great gourmet gift item. Use a small splash of it as a dressing
for fresh fruit salad.*

6 to 8 ripe mangoes
4 cups white rum (1 quart)
Juice of 8 to 10 medium-size limes
8 cups sugar
2 cinnamon sticks
4 cups water (1 quart)

Wash and peel the mangoes. Remove the flesh from the pits and chop the flesh.
Place in a large container. Pour the rum and lime juice over the fruit and allow it
to stand covered for 7 days.

In a bowl, combine the sugar, cinnamon sticks and water and stir well. Pour
over the mango mixture. Allow it to stand covered for 10 more days. Strain it into
bottles.

It will keep indefinitely at room temperature. Serve at room temperature
straight up or over ice.

CLASSIC JAMAICAN RUM PUNCH

This classic formula turns up in all of the written discussions of Jamaican drinks. It's the proportions that matter, so interpret it your own way. I will say that sour equals lime juice and strong equals rum. Sweet could be sugar water or a concentrated juice and weak is water or a light juice.

> 1 part sour
> 2 parts sweet
> 3 parts strong
> 4 parts weak

Mix well and serve over crushed ice.

Yield: You decide.

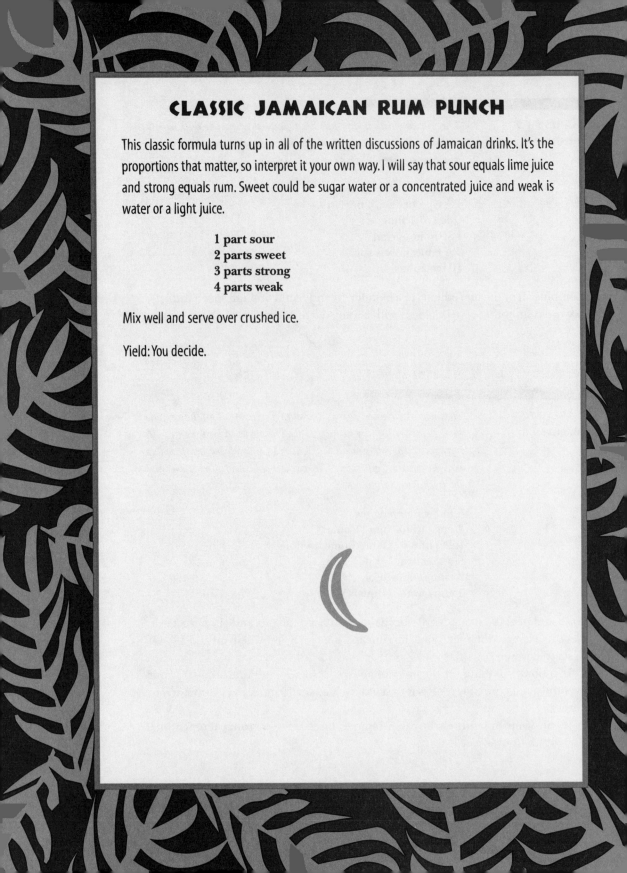

PIMENTO LIQUEUR

MAKES 5 TO 7 QUARTS OF LIQUEUR

The pimento tree is one of the most important flavor cornerstones of Jamaican food. Not only the dried berries, more commonly known as allspice, but its ripe berries, green leaves and wood flavor have both culinary and medicinal preparations.

Unlike most of the recipes in this book, to make this one I'm afraid you'll have to be near a live pimento tree. Also known as Pimento Dram, this recipe from Miss Christiana Lonay, the cook at Oristano in Bluefields, forms the basis for the Oristano cocktail, which blends the liqueur with fresh grapefruit juice.

¼ **pound ripe green pimento berries**
16 cups overproof rum (white rum) (4 quarts)
Juice of 20 limes
16 cups granulated sugar
4 cups water (1 quart)
10 cinnamon sticks

In a large container, soak the ripe pimento berries with 4 cups of the rum and the lime juice for 2 weeks.

Combine the sugar, water and cinnamon sticks in a very large cooking pot. Bring to a boil over high heat and cook until its consistency is a little thinner than honey, 1 to 1½ hours. Strain the pimento mixture and discard the pimento berries. (They can be dried, ground and stored for use as a dry seasoning.) Add the sugar syrup to the pimento liqueur and blend in the remaining 3 quarts of rum. Pour into bottles. It will keep indefinitely at room temperature and is served straight up or over ice.

DRINKS

DESSERTS AND SWEETS

COCONUT CREAM PIE

MAKES 8 SERVINGS

Practically everyone loves coconut cream pie. Made with a real custard filling and meringue on top, this is a sure dessert favorite. If you can't use fresh coconut, shredded, unsweetened coconut in a package will do fine, as will a commercially prepared pie shell.

FOR THE PASTRY
1¼ cups all-purpose flour
⅛ teaspoon salt
¼ cup margarine or lard, chilled (½ stick)
2 tablespoons butter, chilled
3 tablespoons ice-cold water

FOR THE FILLING
½ cup all-purpose flour
½ cup plus 5 tablespoons sugar
⅛ teaspoon salt
2 cups milk
3 eggs, separated
2 tablespoons butter
1 teaspoon vanilla
1 cup plus 1 tablespoon shredded,
   unsweetened coconut

To prepare the pastry, in a large bowl, combine the flour and salt. Cut the margarine and butter into small pieces and add it to the bowl. Working quickly using a knife or pastry blender, cut the flour and fat together until the mixture resembles a coarse meal. Sprinkle the water over the surface, mixing it quickly just until the dough forms a smooth ball. Separate the dough into 2 pieces and flatten them into disks. Refrigerate them until needed.

For the filling, in a bowl that will fit over a pan of boiling water (or a double boiler), combine the flour, ½ cup of sugar and salt. Heat the milk in a heavy saucepan over medium-high until small bubbles appear at the edge of the milk. Using a whisk to stir, pour the scalded milk into the flour mixture and cook over medium heat until it thickens, 2 to 3 minutes.

In a large bowl, whisk together the egg yolks and add 1 tablespoon of the hot custard mixture. Blend well. Whisk the egg yolk mixture into the custard (still on the stove top). Blend in the butter and vanilla. Cook 2 minutes more. Remove the bowl from the heat and let cool, stirring it a couple of times. Fold in 1 cup of the coconut.

Preheat the oven to 400°F. Roll one piece of the chilled dough on a floured surface to a thickness of ⅛ inch and fit it into a 9-inch pie pan (refrigerate the other piece of pastry for another occasion). Fold over edges of the pastry and pinch it all around. Line the pastry with wax paper or foil and weigh it down with dried beans or pebbles. Blind bake the crust for 13 minutes.

Reduce the oven temperature to 350°F. Remove the paper and weights.

In a large bowl, whip the egg whites until stiff. Add the 5 tablespoons of sugar and continue to whip for 2 minutes until it is glossy and peaks stand up when the beater is removed (stiff peaks are formed).

Spoon the custard filling into the cooked pie crust. Smooth it out evenly. Spread the meringue over the filling. Bake for 10 to 15 minutes or until the meringue is lightly browned.

NOTE The meringue will cut more easily if the knife is dipped in warm water before making each slice.

VARIATION

To make Banana Cream Pie, omit the coconut from the custard and place 2 sliced ripe bananas on top of the custard.

PINEAPPLE PIE

MAKES 8 SERVINGS   *Jamaican pineapple pie is a local alternative to the traditional British and American apple pie. It's usually spiced with nutmeg and cinnamon, but in this recipe, ginger is the featured spice.*

FOR THE FILLING
1 pineapple
⅔ cup sugar
½ teaspoon ground ginger
1 tablespoon fresh lime juice
1 tablespoon dark rum
½ teaspoon salt
¾ cup all-purpose flour
¼ cup water
2 tablespoons butter

FOR THE PASTRY
1¼ cups all-purpose flour
¼ cup shredded, unsweetened coconut (optional)
¼ teaspoon salt
¼ cup margarine or lard, chilled (½ stick)
2 tablespoons butter, chilled
¼ cup cold water
1 egg, beaten, combined with 1 teaspoon water

Core the pineapple by slicing the peeled fruit into quarters lengthwise. Slice the core off each piece. (Reserve the peel and core for Pineappleade, page 111.) Chop the pineapple into approximately ¾-inch-square pieces. In a medium-size saucepan, combine the pineapple with the sugar, ginger, lime juice, rum, salt, flour and water. Cook over medium heat until thickened, about 5 minutes. Remove from the heat and stir in the butter. Let sit until cooled completely.

Meanwhile, to prepare the pastry, in a large bowl, combine the flour, coconut and salt. Cut the margarine and butter into small pieces and add to the bowl. Working lightly with a knife, pastry blender or your fingers, cut the flour and fat together until the mixture resembles a coarse meal. Sprinkle the water over the surface, mixing it quickly just until the dough forms a smooth ball. Separate into 2 disks and chill in the refrigerator until needed.

Preheat the oven to 375°F. Roll out one piece of the pastry and line the bottom of a 9-inch pie plate with it. Pour the cooled pineapple mixture into the pie shell. Roll out the other piece of pastry and cover the fruit. Trim the top pastry so it overlaps the bottom. Roll and pinch the edges until sealed. Make a couple of slits in the pastry and brush the pastry with the egg/water wash. Bake the pie for 45 minutes or until the crust is golden brown.

VARIATION

For a more traditional pie, add ½ teaspoon ground cinnamon and ¼ teaspoon ground nutmeg to the pineapple and other ingredients.

SWEET POTATO PIE

MAKES 8 SERVINGS

Similar to American pumpkin pie, this pie is also made in Jamaica without a crust. This recipe also works well using mashed pumpkin instead of sweet potatoes. Serve it topped with whipped cream, vanilla ice cream or honey-sweetened yogurt.

¾ **pound sweet potatoes (1½ cups cooked and mashed)**

FOR THE PASTRY
1¼ **cups all-purpose flour**
¼ **teaspoon salt**
¼ **cup margarine or lard, chilled (½ stick)**
2 **tablespoons butter, chilled**
¼ **cup cold water**

FOR THE FILLING
½ **cup dark brown sugar**
1 **teaspoon cinnamon**
½ **teaspoon ground ginger**
Dash nutmeg
¼ **teaspoon salt**
2 **cups milk or milk substitute**
3 **eggs**

Preheat the oven to 400°F. Bake the sweet potatoes for 1 hour or until completely soft. (Or you may boil the potatoes in a large pot of water.) Remove from the heat. When cool enough to handle, peel and mash the potatoes.

To prepare the pastry, in a large bowl, combine the flour and salt. Cut the margarine and butter into small pieces and add it to the bowl. Working lightly with a knife, a pastry blender or your fingertips, cut the flour and fat together until the mixture resembles a coarse meal. Sprinkle the water over the surface, mixing quickly just until the dough forms a smooth ball. Separate it into 2 pieces, reserving one for another use. (It will keep in the refrigerator up to 2 weeks.)

Roll out the pastry and place it into a 9-inch pie plate. Pinch around the edges of the crust. Set aside.

In a large bowl, combine the sweet potato puree and brown sugar. Stir in the cinnamon, ginger, nutmeg and salt. In a separate bowl, lightly beat the milk and eggs together. Blend it into the sweet potato mixture until combined.

Pour the sweet potato filling into the pie shell. Bake the pie for 10 minutes at 400°F. Then reduce the heat to 350°F and bake 30 to 40 minutes longer or until the custard is set.

VARIATION
Fold chopped, candied ginger into the filling for a different taste.

BANANA CAKE

MAKES 8 SERVINGS   *A crispy brown sugar and butter topping elevates this moist and delicious cake above most ordinary recipes.*

2 cups all-purpose flour
½ teaspoon baking soda
¾ teaspoon salt
¾ cup sugar
½ cup margarine, melted (1 stick)
½ cup buttermilk, yogurt or milk
2 eggs
1 teaspoon vanilla
2 ripe bananas, mashed (about 1 cup)

FOR THE TOPPING
¼ cup all-purpose flour
¼ cup dark brown sugar
¼ cup butter (½ stick)

Preheat the oven to 300°F. In a large bowl, combine the flour, baking soda, salt and sugar. Blend in the margarine, mixing together until moist. Add ¼ cup of the buttermilk and combine.

In a separate bowl, combine the other ¼ cup of buttermilk with the eggs and blend into the flour mixture. Add the vanilla and mashed bananas. Beat for 1 minute. Place the batter in a greased 9×13×2-inch pan.

To make the topping, squeeze the flour, brown sugar and butter together with your hands. Crumble the topping evenly over the batter. Bake for 35 to 40 minutes. When the cake is done, an inserted toothpick or fork should come out clean from the center.

NOTE Buttermilk is the preferred liquid for this recipe, but it is equally successful with a combination of milk and plain yogurt or with milk alone.

PINEAPPLE UPSIDE-DOWN CAKE

MAKES 8 SERVINGS

This old-fashioned cake cooked in a cast-iron skillet remains one of my favorite desserts. The canned pineapple will work but doesn't come close to the heavenly flavor of a fresh, ripe "pine" combined with butter and brown sugar.

1⅓ cups all-purpose flour
¾ cup sugar
2 teaspoons baking powder
½ teaspoon salt
¼ cup vegetable oil
¾ cup milk
1 teaspoon vanilla
1 egg
1 lime, grated rind
1 tablespoon fresh lime juice
¼ cup butter (½ stick)
½ cup dark brown sugar
1 fresh, ripe pineapple or one 20-ounce
    can pineapple slices
15 pecans

Preheat the oven to 350°F. In a mixing bowl, sift together the flour, sugar, baking powder and salt. Add the oil and milk to the bowl and beat for 1 minute. Add the vanilla, egg, lime rind and lime juice, blending just until well combined.

In a cast-iron skillet over medium heat, melt the butter. Remove from the heat and sprinkle the brown sugar around the skillet. Arrange the pineapple slices and pecans on top. Pour the batter evenly over top and bake for 45 minutes.

Remove from the oven and cool the cake in the pan for 5 minutes. Turn the cake out onto a circular platter.

BANANA CUSTARD

**MAKES 6 TO 8
SERVINGS**

This is an old-time recipe. Bananas have played a dominant role in the evolution of Jamaican cooking. An export crop and key player in the history of Jamaican commerce, there are twenty varieties of bananas that exist on the island.

**6 ripe bananas
Juice of ½ lime
¾ teaspoon ground nutmeg
3 cups milk
5 tablespoons sugar
3 eggs
½ teaspoon vanilla
1 cup plain bread crumbs**

Preheat the oven to 325°F. In a large bowl, peel and mash the bananas and mix with the lime juice and ½ teaspoon of the nutmeg.

In a saucepan over medium heat, warm the milk and sugar. In a small bowl, blend the eggs and vanilla together, then combine with the banana mixture and milk mixture. Sprinkle the bread crumbs over the buttered baking pan. Pour the custard into a 9×13×2-inch ovenproof dish.

Sprinkle on the remaining ¼ teaspoon of nutmeg. Place the pan into a larger pan that is filled with warm water, ½ inch up the side. Bake for 1 hour or until the custard is set.

BREAD PUDDING
WITH RUM SAUCE

MAKES 8 SERVINGS *This dessert is a great way to use up stale bread, but it is so good you might just buy fresh bread especially to make it. Serve with a scoop of mango ice cream.*

FOR THE PUDDING
¼ cup raisins
2 tablespoons dark rum
12 slices white bread, preferably slightly stale
  (about ½ pound)
1 cup milk
1 cup coconut milk
2 eggs
¾ cup sugar
½ teaspoon vanilla
½ teaspoon cinnamon
¼ teaspoon ground nutmeg

FOR THE SAUCE
¾ cup dark brown sugar
⅓ cup water
½ cup butter (1 stick)
¼ cup dark rum

Preheat the oven to 350°F. Grease a 9×13×2-inch ovenproof baking dish. In a small bowl, combine the raisins and rum and set aside.

Remove the crusts from the bread. In a blender or food processor, blend the crusts into bread crumbs. Set aside 3 tablespoons and reserve the rest for another use. Cube the bread and put the pieces into a large bowl. Pour the milk and coconut milk over the bread. Set aside to saturate completely.

In a separate bowl, beat together the eggs, sugar, vanilla, cinnamon and nutmeg. Pour it over the bread along with the raisins and rum. Stir the mixture until well blended. Pour it into the baking dish and sprinkle the 3 tablespoons of bread crumbs over the top. Bake for 40 minutes.

Meanwhile, prepare the sauce. In a small saucepan, combine the brown sugar, water, butter and rum. Bring to a boil over medium-high heat and boil gently until thickened, about 10 minutes. Pour a little over each portion when serving.

DUCKANOO

**MAKES 10 TO 12
PIECES
(6 TO 10 SERVINGS)**

This is a kind of pudding made of "starch" food such as plantain, green banana, cassava or cornmeal wrapped in a banana leaf. It is known in Jamaica by its many names (dokono, dokunu, blue drawers and tie-a-leaf), which are firmly rooted in the African tradition. In Ghana, for instance, there is a preparation called dokon, which closely resembles Jamaica's dokuno.

2 cups yellow, fine or coarse cornmeal
½ cup sugar
½ teaspoon cinnamon
½ teaspoon ground ginger
¼ teaspoon ground nutmeg
½ teaspoon salt
⅓ cup shredded, unsweetened coconut
1⅓ cups coconut milk
½ teaspoon vanilla
Banana leaves

In a large bowl, combine the cornmeal, sugar, cinnamon, ginger, nutmeg and salt. Mix in the shredded coconut. Blend in the coconut milk and vanilla.

Cut the banana leaves into large rectangles (peeling off 20 long strings for tying). Pass each leaf through a pot of boiling water to soften it before putting a large spoonful of the cornmeal mixture in the center. Gently roll it up and turn over both ends. Using a piece of the string, tie it in both directions like a parcel.

Repeat the process until the filling is used up. Stack the parcels into a steamer and cook for 1 hour. Or drop them into a pot of boiling water and cook for 1 hour.

GREEN BANANA PUDDING

MAKES 6 SERVINGS   *Serve this pudding during the holidays topped with Hard Sauce (page 106).*

½ cup butter (1 stick)
1 cup sugar
1 egg
½ cup milk
1 teaspoon vanilla
½ cup all-purpose flour
1 teaspoon baking powder
⅛ teaspoon ground nutmeg
1 cup green banana, finely grated
¾ cup chopped, candied fruit

Preheat the oven to 300°F. In a large bowl, cream together the butter and sugar. Beat in the egg. Add the milk and vanilla and blend thoroughly. Stir in the flour, baking powder and nutmeg. Fold in the green banana and candied fruit.

Place the pudding into an 8-inch square, ovenproof dish and place it in a larger pan filled with hot water, ½ inch up the sides. Cover the pan with foil. Place in a 300°F oven and steam the pudding for 1 hour. Check to be sure the water hasn't evaporated after 30 minutes. Add more water if necessary.

Serve a spoonful of the Hard Sauce over each serving.

SWEET POTATO PUDDING

MAKES 6 TO 8 SERVINGS

Sweet potato is often referred to as "potato" and the nonsweet version as "Irish potato" or simply "Irish." Sometimes "yam" is used to describe a sweet potato, which is an entirely different white or yellow nonsweet tuber in Jamaica.

Used in many forms, the nutritious and versatile sweet potato is an important staple item in the Caribbean diet. This recipe can be used both as a dessert and a side dish for the main meal. The subtle coconut milk complements the smooth texture of the sweet potato.

2 pounds sweet potatoes (6 medium size)
⅓ cup raisins
¼ cup sugar
3 cups coconut milk
½ teaspoon vanilla
½ teaspoon cinnamon
½ teaspoon ground ginger
¼ teaspoon ground nutmeg
¼ cup shredded, unsweetened coconut

Preheat the oven to 350°F. Peel and grate the raw sweet potatoes into a large bowl. Mix in the raisins. Stir in the sugar, coconut milk, vanilla, cinnamon, ginger, nutmeg and coconut. Grease a 9×13×2-inch ovenproof dish and pour in the sweet potato mixture. Bake for 1 hour. It is best served warm.

COCONUT BREAD

**MAKES 1 LOAF
OR 8 SLICES**

Serve this sliced and toasted with butter and Pineapple Jam (page 107) for a special breakfast treat.

1½ cups all-purpose flour
2 teaspoons baking powder
½ teaspoon salt
½ cup sugar
1 egg, lightly beaten
1 teaspoon vanilla
½ cup milk
½ cup grated dried coconut

Preheat the oven to 350°F. In a bowl, combine the flour, baking powder, salt and sugar. Add the egg and vanilla and mix. Add the milk and coconut and mix until well combined. Put in a small greased loaf pan. Bake for 1 hour or until the bread is springy to the touch. Remove from the oven and let cool in the pan for 5 minutes. Turn the bread out onto a wire rack to cool before slicing.

VARIATION
For a more concentrated flavor, use coconut milk in place of the regular milk.

GINGERBREAD

MAKES 8 SERVINGS

Ginger is one of the most used spices in the Jamaican household, both for cooking and medicinal folk remedies. The smell of ginger-bread cooking in the house conjures up warm memories for many people.

1½ cups all-purpose flour
1 teaspoon baking soda
¼ teaspoon salt
2 teaspoons ground ginger
½ cup dark brown sugar
¾ cup molasses
¾ cup margarine or butter (1½ sticks)
2 eggs
¼ cup milk

Preheat the oven to 300°F. In a large mixing bowl, sift together the flour, baking soda, salt and ginger.

In a medium-size saucepan, combine the brown sugar, molasses and margarine. Place over low heat. Cook it until the sugar dissolves. Remove from the heat and cool without letting it harden. In a separate bowl, combine the eggs and milk. Add it to the cooled molasses mixture and blend it until well combined. Slowly add this mixture to the flour and mix well.

Line a greased 8-inch round cake pan with wax paper and pour the mixture into it. Bake for 1 hour and 15 minutes or until a toothpick or fork inserted into the center comes out clean.

VARIATION

Add 2 ounces each of chopped nuts and/or chopped, candied ginger, which is an excellent digestive aid.

MANGO BREAD

**MAKES 1 LOAF
OR 8 SERVINGS**

Any excuse to use a mango is fine with me. Here the subtle ginger taste enhances the mango flavor without overpowering it. It smells like candy when it's cooking. This is a great choice for tea time.

1½ cups all-purpose flour
½ teaspoon baking soda
½ teaspoon baking powder
½ teaspoon salt
1 teaspoon ground ginger
½ cup dark brown sugar
¼ cup sugar
½ cup margarine, melted (1 stick)
2 to 3 small, ripe mangoes, peeled, pitted and diced
    (1 cup)
2 eggs, beaten

Preheat the oven to 350°F. In a large bowl, combine the flour, baking soda, baking powder, salt and ginger. Mix in the brown and white sugars. Add the margarine, mango and eggs to the flour mixture and blend well.

Put the batter into a small, greased loaf pan and bake for 30 to 40 minutes or until the top springs back when touched and is lightly golden.

PUMPKIN BREAD

**MAKES 1 LOAF
OR 8 SERVINGS**

Although this quick bread is best prepared with freshly steamed West Indian pumpkin, American or canned pumpkin is an acceptable substitute.

1½ **cups all-purpose flour**
½ **teaspoon baking soda**
½ **teaspoon baking powder**
½ **teaspoon salt**
½ **teaspoon ground cinnamon**
½ **cup vegetable oil**
¾ **cup dark brown sugar**
1 **cup pumpkin puree**
1 **egg, beaten**
⅓ **cup raisins (optional)**

Preheat the oven to 350°F. In a medium-size bowl, sift together the flour, baking soda, baking powder, salt and cinnamon.

In the bowl of a electric mixer (or a large bowl), beat together the oil, brown sugar and pumpkin until well combined. Add the egg and blend well. Add the raisins and mix. Blend in the flour mixture. Turn the mixture into a well-greased loaf pan and bake for 45 minutes or until a toothpick or fork inserted into the center comes out clean. Remove the bread from the pan and allow to cool on a wire rack.

NOTE This freezes well.

VARIATION

For an extra zip, add some freshly grated orange rind with the pumpkin.

COCONUT COOKIES

MAKES 2 DOZEN COOKIES

These cookies make a lovely dessert paired with fresh fruit.

½ cup butter (1 stick)
½ cup sugar
1 teaspoon vanilla
1 egg, beaten
1½ cups all-purpose flour
1 teaspoon baking powder
¼ teaspoon salt
1 cup shredded, unsweetened coconut

Preheat the oven to 350°F. In a large bowl, cream together the butter, sugar and vanilla. Add the egg and mix just until combined. In a separate bowl, combine the flour, baking powder, salt and coconut. Blend it into the butter mixture.

   Place small spoonfuls of batter onto a greased cookie sheet and bake for 14 minutes or until the edges are golden. Remove the cookies from the cookie sheet immediately and allow them to cool on a rack.

VARIATION
For chocolate fans, fold in ¼ cup chopped bittersweet chocolate.

JACKASS CORN

MAKES 12 TO 15 BISCUITS

This crunchy snack will keep for a long time. Yet another clever Jamaican expression, its name reputedly comes from the sounds made during eating, which resemble a jackass chewing on his corn.

1 cup all-purpose flour
¼ teaspoon baking soda
1 cup sugar
½ teaspoon ground nutmeg
¼ teaspoon salt
1 cup shredded, unsweetened coconut
3 tablespoons water

Preheat the oven to 375°F. In a medium-size bowl, combine the flour, baking soda, sugar, nutmeg and salt. Stir in the coconut. Add the water and mix, forming a very stiff dough that will not crumble.

Roll out the dough on a floured board to ⅛ inch thick. Cut the dough into small rectangles. Place the pieces onto a greased cookie sheet and prick each one with a fork. Bake for 8 to 9 minutes or until brown. Remove from the oven and transfer to a plate to cool.

TOTOES

Another Jamaican sweety, these spicy coconut squares make great afternoon snacks along with a glass of Limeade (page 110).

3 cups all-purpose flour
3 teaspoons baking powder
1 teaspoon cinnamon
¼ teaspoon ground nutmeg
½ teaspoon salt
2 cups sugar
½ cup butter, melted (1 stick)
½ cup milk
2 eggs, beaten
2 cups shredded, unsweetened coconut

Preheat the oven to 375°F. In a large bowl, sift together the flour, baking powder, cinnamon, nutmeg and salt. Blend in the sugar and butter. Add the milk and eggs and mix. When the mixture is well combined, add the coconut.

Grease a 9 × 13 × 2-inch Pyrex™ baking dish and smooth the batter evenly into the dish. Bake for 50 to 60 minutes. Remove from the oven. When the cake is cooled, cut it into squares.

BULLAS

**MAKES 12–16
ROUNDS**

These are like Totoes—only without coconut. Bullas have long been a beloved afternoon snack, available at bakeries and snack counters.

**3 cups all-purpose flour
1 teaspoon baking powder
½ teaspoon baking soda
½ teaspoon nutmeg
½ teaspoon ground allspice (dry pimento berries)
1 teaspoon ground ginger
½ teaspoon salt
1 cup dark brown sugar
¼ cup water
3 tablespoons butter, melted**

Preheat the oven to 325°F. In a large bowl, sift together the flour, baking powder, baking soda, nutmeg, allspice, ginger and salt. In a small saucepan, combine the brown sugar and water and cook over low heat until the sugar dissolves and is a syrupy consistency. Add it along with the butter to the flour mixture and mix until combined. Knead the dough with your hands a few times.

Roll it out on a floured surface and cut out ¼-inch-thick rounds. Place the rounds on a greased cookie sheet and bake for 20 to 30 minutes. Remove from the oven. Cool on a rack or plate.

PUMPKIN GRIZZADAS WITH YAM PASTRY

Classic grizzadas are coconut-filled tarts. This recipe, adapted from an old Jamaican newspaper clipping, replaces the coconut with pumpkin and adds yam to the pastry. For the adventurous, it's a unique alternative. For purists, simply replace the pumpkin with grated coconut. With its history of sugarcane production, Jamaica is a nation of "sweet tooths," and grizzadas are eaten as snacks.

FOR THE FILLING
1 pound pumpkin, peeled and cubed
3 tablespoons sugar
2 tablespoons fresh lime juice
1 teaspoon ground ginger
½ teaspoon cinnamon
1 teaspoon vanilla
1 egg, beaten

FOR THE PASTRY
½ pound yam, peeled and cubed
1 teaspoon margarine
1 teaspoon milk

Preheat the oven to 350°F. In large pots, boil the pumpkin and yam (for the pastry) separately until they are each tender. In a large bowl, crush the cooked pumpkin and combine it with the sugar, lime juice, ginger, cinnamon, vanilla and egg. Put the pumpkin mixture in a saucepan and cook over low heat until it begins to thicken, about 5 minutes. Set aside to cool.

Meanwhile, to make the pastry, in a large bowl, crush the cooked yam with the margarine and milk. Knead it just until combined. With floured hands, separate the pastry into 6 pieces. Shape each piece into a ball, flatten slightly into a circle, and press a small indentation in the center. Fill each one with a spoonful of the pumpkin mixture and bake on a greased cookie sheet for 12 to 15 minutes.

PLANTAIN TARTS

MAKES 8 TARTS

These snacks are a favorite of Jamaican children and can be found at any local patty shop or at an after-school vendor cart.

FOR THE PASTRY
1¼ cups all-purpose flour
1 teaspoon salt
1 teaspoon cinnamon
¼ teaspoon ground nutmeg
½ cup margarine or butter, chilled (1 stick)
¼ cup butter, chilled (½ stick)
3 tablespoons ice-cold water

FOR THE FILLING
4 very ripe plantains
4 tablespoons butter
½ cup plus 2 tablespoons sugar
¾ teaspoon ground nutmeg
2 teaspoons vanilla
¼ cup water
½ cup raisins

For the pastry, in a large mixing bowl, combine the flour, salt, cinnamon and nutmeg. Cut the margarine and butter into small pieces and add it to the bowl. Working quickly using a knife, pastry blender or your fingertips, work the flour mixture, margarine and butter together until it resembles a very coarse meal. Add the water to the bowl. With floured hands, mix and squeeze the dough just until it forms a ball. Knead once or twice to fully combine it (the less the better). Separate the dough into 2 pieces, flattening each into a thick pancake. Wrap individually and refrigerate for at least 30 minutes.

For the filling, cut the plantains in half and cook them in a pot of boiling water for 10 minutes. Remove the plantains to a bowl. Peel and mash them along with the butter. Put in a saucepan along with ½ cup of the sugar, nutmeg, vanilla and water. Stir and cook over medium heat for 3 minutes. Mix in the raisins and remove it from the heat. Allow to cool completely.

Preheat the oven to 400°F. Take both pieces of the dough and roll it out on a floured surface one at a time. Cut out eight 5-inch-round shapes. Spread some plantain filling over one side of each shape and fold over the pastry, crimping the edges with a fork. Sprinkle the remaining 2 tablespoons of sugar over the top of each tart and bake for 15 minutes.

BAKED BANANAS

MAKES 2 SERVINGS

Nothing melts in the mouth like baked bananas. Served with any kind of cream topping, it is a simple, unsurpassed dessert. Adjust the ingredients and flavors to your personal taste.

2 bananas
Juice of 1 lime
1 tablespoon dark rum
¼ teaspoon ground cinnamon
⅛ teaspoon ground nutmeg
1 tablespoon dark brown sugar
1 tablespoon butter (optional)

Preheat the oven to 400°F. Peel the bananas and slice in half lengthwise. Lay the pieces into a buttered 9×13×2-inch ovenproof dish. Pour the lime juice and rum evenly over the bananas. Sprinkle on the cinnamon, nutmeg and brown sugar. Dot on the butter, if using, and bake for 10 to 15 minutes. Serve hot, topped with a tablespoon of fresh cream or ice cream.

FROZEN LIME SUCK-SUCK

MAKES 6 TO 8 SUCK-SUCKS

The enterprising cook at Woodstock Farm, Miss Lammie, who at one time produced some of the best homemade guava jelly sold in Jamaica, packages these frozen sweets and sells them to the workers on the cattle ranch.

Juice of 6 limes
6 cups water
1 cup sugar

In a large pitcher, combine the lime juice and 5 cups of the water in a large pitcher. In a pot, combine the sugar with the remaining cup of water and place over low heat until the sugar is dissolved. Add the sugar water to the lime juice and let sit until cooled completely. Pour the liquid into small plastic bags, tie the top securely and freeze. Cut off a corner of the bag before serving.

BROILED
GRAPEFRUIT

MAKES 6 SERVINGS   *The grapefruit's tart flavor is a nice way to clean the palate after a large meal.*

3 grapefruits
2 tablespoons dark brown sugar

Halve each grapefruit and carve around each section in every half. Sprinkle a teaspoon of brown sugar over each half. Broil until the sugar is bubbling. Serve immediately.

COCONUT
ICE CREAM

MAKES 1 QUART   *Many of Jamaica's delicious fruits can be used in place of coconut for this homestyle ice cream. It has a great creamy consistency.*

1 coconut
4 cups boiling water
½ seven-ounce can sweetened condensed milk
½ teaspoon vanilla
2 tablespoons rum

Crack the hard outer shell of the coconut with a hammer. Separate the flesh from the shell. Shred the flesh in a blender, food processor or with a cheese grater. Pour 4 cups of the hot or boiling water over the grated coconut and let stand for 5 minutes. Pour it through a fine mesh strainer into a large freezerproof bowl. Squeeze the remaining milk out of the flesh.

Add the condensed milk, vanilla and rum and mix. Put in the freezer and stir it a couple of times as it freezes.

VARIATIONS
Mango Ice Cream: Blend the flesh of 2 ripe mangoes with enough water to make 3 cups of puree. Substitute the puree for the coconut milk.
Banana Ice Cream: Blend 2 to 3 bananas in a blender with enough milk to make 3 cups of puree. Substitute the puree for the coconut milk.

BANANA FRITTERS

MAKES 6 SERVINGS

Banana fritters are another childhood favorite of mine, and my children now adore these too—along with almost anyone else who tries them. Following a plate of fresh fruit, these easy fritters make a fantastic breakfast.

6 ripe bananas
2 eggs, beaten
¾ cup all-purpose flour
3 tablespoons vegetable oil

In a large bowl, mash the bananas and blend in the eggs. Stir in the flour. Heat the oil in a large skillet over medium-high heat until hot. Drop spoonfuls (2 to 3 inches in diameter) of the batter into the hot oil. Reduce the heat to medium. When bubbles begin to appear, turn and cook the other side until golden brown. Repeat the process until all the batter is used up, keeping the cooked fritters in a warm oven. Serve them with maple syrup or honey.

PUMPKIN FRITTERS

**MAKES 12
SILVER-DOLLAR–SIZE
PANCAKES,
OR 4 SERVINGS**

These tasty morsels have a soft, yet dense and chewy texture. They're a big hit with the kids. Pair the fritters up with fresh grapefruit or ugli fruit for breakfast. Serve each fritter straight off the skillet, sprinkled with brown sugar.

½ pound pumpkin, peeled and chopped (about 1 cup)
1 tablespoon sugar
½ teaspoon cinnamon
⅔ cup all-purpose flour
½ teaspoon baking soda
½ cup milk
2 tablespoons vegetable oil
¼ cup dark brown sugar

Steam the pumpkin in a steamer basket over simmering water until soft, about 8 minutes. Put the pumpkin in a medium-size bowl and mash until smooth. Add the sugar and cinnamon and stir.

In another bowl, sift together the flour and baking soda and add it to the pumpkin mixture. Stir until well combined. Slowly whisk in the milk. You should end up with a thick pourable batter.

In a large skillet, heat half of the oil over medium-high heat until it is very hot. Pour ⅛ cup of the batter on the skillet for each fritter.

When the batter on top is bubbling, flip the fritter over and cook until golden on the other side. Using the remaining oil, repeat until all the batter is used up. Sprinkle each fritter with brown sugar before serving.

CORNMEAL PORRIDGE

**MAKES 4 TO 6
SERVINGS**

Many different versions of this mainstay breakfast are eaten throughout Jamaica, especially by children.

**1 coconut
4 cups boiling water
2 cups water
2 bay leaves
1 small cinnamon stick
2 cups yellow, coarse or fine cornmeal
Two 12-ounce cans evaporated milk
3 drops vanilla
¼ cup sugar**

Crack the hard outer shell of the coconut with a hammer. Separate the flesh from the shell. Shred the flesh in a blender, food processor or with a cheese grater. Pour the 4 cups of boiling water over the grated coconut and let it stand for 5 minutes. Pour into a bowl through a fine mesh strainer. Squeeze the remaining milk out of the flesh.

In a large pot, combine the coconut milk, 2 cups water, bay leaves and cinnamon stick. Over high heat, slowly stir in the cornmeal and bring the mixture to a boil, stirring until it thickens, 3 to 4 minutes. Reduce the heat to low and simmer for 10 to 15 minutes.

Stir in the evaporated milk, vanilla and sugar and cook for an additional 5 minutes. Water can be used to thin it if desired. It can be served hot or cold. The taste improves with age. It will keep in the refrigerator for 4 days.

PEANUT PORRIDGE
WITH MOLASSES

**MAKES 6 TO 8
SERVINGS**

*Every weekday morning on a street corner in the Liguanea section
of Kingston, where vast fields of mango trees once graced the
Liguanea plains in place of today's bustling cityscape, a Rastaman
serves this porridge from a large vat that sits over an open fire.*

*Folks pull over in their cars, holding out a coffee cup or pail.
Others step up on the curb and get a plastic cup full of the porridge
topped with molasses. A colorful group of characters surrounds
the area and converses warmly with the peanut porridge man while
casually sipping their breakfast porridge. With a kind smile, his
dreads piled high in his tam, the Rastaman serves as many as the
pot will feed, then heads home after a day's work well done.*

This recipe was decoded by taste and adapted for home cooking.

**2 cups shelled peanuts (unsalted), ground
2 cups hominy, canned or soaked
4 cups coconut milk
1 cinnamon stick
4 to 6 allspice berries (dry pimento berries)
¼ cup molasses**

Combine all of the ingredients except molasses in a large cooking pot and mix
them well. Place over medium heat and simmer for 20 minutes. Serve in a mug
with a tablespoon of molasses on each serving.

INDEX